CAMRA
CAMPAIGN FOR REAL ALE

Berkshire pub guide

a comprehensive guide to Real Ale in the Royal County of Berkshire

Contact us

Do you have any comments on this guide?
Would you like to receive free updates to this guide?
See page 135 for details.

Credits

Editor: Colin Lanham
Assistant editors: Norman Spalding, John Dearing
Branch co-ordination: Vic Powell, Mike Smith, Colin Lanham
Database management: Norman Spalding
Advertising: Derek Woodacre, Colin Lanham, John Robinson
Front cover: Dave McKerchar and Sophie Watson
Maps: Sophie Watson (town maps), Rob Tough (county map)
Desktop publishing assistance: Fenton Wallace
Proof-reading: Phil Ashling, Martyn Bramble, Sandie Brown, Allan Conner, John Dearing, Dave McKerchar, Vic Powell, Mike Smith, Norman Spalding, Fenton Wallace, Sophie Watson
Town descriptions: Dave McKerchar
Surveys: Brian Allen, Mike Avery, Jeff Ball, Louise & Mike Beardmore, Janet & John Blurton, Dave Bolton, Sandie Brown, Andy Church, Gus Clark, Allan Conner, Brian Coombes, John Dearing, Jeremy Dickins, Alasdair Donaldson, Rob Ellis, Tony Fox Griffiths, Peter George, Terri Goddard, Richard Goss, Geoff Grayer, John Hopper, Ian Hill, Peter Jackson, Bob Keegan, Colin Lanham, Richard Lock, Dave McKerchar, John McKeown, Ian Mihell, Laurie Mountjoy, Vic Powell, Mo Quirke, John Robinson, Carmel Smith, Mike Smith, Pete Smith, Norman Spalding, Clive Stevens, Les Taylor, Jeff Ward, Dave Withers, Russ Wood, Rob Wright, Jeff Yalden

Designed and typeset by Sophie Watson, a student in the Department of Typography & Graphic Communication at The University of Reading.

Printed in Great Britain by Albert Gait Ltd, Grimsby.

Special thanks to Mick Stocks and the staff of the Department of Typography & Graphic Communication at The University of Reading. Also to Roy Golding, editor of the Surrey Pub Guide, and Peter Jackson for services above and beyond the call of duty.

ISBN 1-85249-156-6

Welcome!

Welcome to the sixth edition of the *Berkshire Pub Guide*, produced by the Berkshire branches of CAMRA, the Campaign for Real Ale.

The Royal County is home to many hundreds of excellent pubs waiting to be discovered, ranging from large bustling town centre establishments to some wonderful historic country pubs; from the small Victorian alehouse to the old village coaching inn. Among the hostelries to be sampled are (reputedly) England's third oldest inn; numerous establishments associated with famous historical events; and two pubs which have achieved the accolade of being listed on CAMRA's National Inventory of Heritage Pubs for their almost totally unspoilt condition.

An exciting recent innovation is the revival of the home-brew pub, a concept that had mostly died out in the nineteenth century; Berkshire now has five such establishments. But perhaps the best news of all is the fact that roughly eighty percent of the county's pubs now sell traditional British beer; a marked improvement on the situation when the first Berkshire guide was published in 1975 when only thirty-odd percent of houses were offering the real thing.

So if so many pubs are now selling real ale, why the need for a new real ale pub guide? Well, several reasons really...

Firstly, if four out of five pubs sells traditional beer then it figures that one in five do not and these establishments are best avoided by the discerning drinker.

Next, although virtually all real beer is preferable to the factory processed variety, many people believe that the beers produced by the small independent brewers and microbrewers have more character and flavour than most of the products produced by the large national companies. This guide points the way to many of these excellent beers.

Then there is the question of quality. Real beer is a living commodity requiring an amount of skill and care to serve in top condition. Not all establishments give a priority to this important part of their business, or they may employ dubious practices when storing or serving their beers (such as those explained further on). So again, the beer you drink (and pay for) may not be served in the way you would prefer. For this reason, for the first time, a new category of 'specially recommended' pubs has been introduced where the beer is most likely to be served in top condition in an efficient and friendly manner.

Whether you are a resident seeking out a new watering-hole or a visitor exploring the many delights the county has to offer, the *Berkshire Pub Guide* is the essential companion when searching for the perfect pint and a warm welcome in an excellent pub.

COLIN LANHAM
Editor

How this guide is compiled

CAMRA is the beer lovers' organisation and, not surprisingly, many of its members regularly visit the pubs throughout the county, either individually or as part of their branches' social activities.

In order to collect the information contained within this guide, however, a number of volunteers from each of the county's local branches visited each pub unannounced to carry out a survey. This exercise was completed over a six-month period to May 1999. As with all CAMRA local guides, advertising is not accepted from individual pubs and no inducements, either financial or otherwise, are accepted to influence the listing in this publication.

There are three types of entry in this guide. Pubs found to be selling no real ale simply receive a statement to that effect. All pubs serving traditional beer receive a full description. Those pubs which, when surveyed, were found to be providing excellent beer and service, are classed as 'recommended' and receive a full listing of their facilities. This does not necessarily suggest that those not recommended are not worth a visit. For a number of real ale pubs, interesting historical information is also provided.

An industry in turmoil

If anybody feels that CAMRA has done its job and the future of real ale is safe then the events which took place in the three weeks prior to this guide going to press should serve as a warning.

First came the news that Whitbread, having recently closed Flowers' brewery in Cheltenham, were looking to get out of brewing altogether (after more than 260 years). This was swiftly followed by a £2.4 billion deal to buy all of Allied Domecq's pubs which confirmed the story and puts the future of their remaining breweries in serious doubt.

The next bombshell was the news that Scottish Courage were to close their Bristol brewery, after saying in 1997 when they took it over that its future was safe. This brewery was established in 1702 and is the world's largest dedicated real ale brewery. Their 'reason' is the decline in sales of Courage Best and Directors. Not surprising when their cask ales have been starved of vital advertising. In the previous six-month period the company spent £3.6 million promoting keg and tinned versions of John Smith's while at the same time the Courage brands received a pathetic £5000.

But perhaps the most bitter pill to swallow is the news that local brewer Morland (established 1711) has opened discussions to be taken over by Greene King. This is the same Morland who (with CAMRA's considerable assistance) fought off a hostile bid from the same Greene King in 1992. Instead of steadily building on this success the company seems to have over-stretched itself with numerous pub acquisitions but without much regard for producing a top notch range of ales, with only Old Speckled Hen recognised as a winner.

In 1997 Morland made few friends when they bought the famous Ruddles Rutland brewery (founded 1858) and promptly closed it, transferring production to Abingdon. A major upgrading of the Abingdon brewery in 1998 costing £5 million obviously signals its imminent closure, which will surely be its fate if the Greene King deal goes ahead.

If this madness continues, not only will the heritage and traditions of Britain be severely damaged but also quality and choice will be sacrificed in favour of blandness and uniformity, made inevitable by the mass production and promotion favoured by the few mega-corporations left manufacturing beer in any quantity in this country in a few years' time.

If ever there was a time to join CAMRA, surely it must be now.

What is real ale?

Traditional British Beer (or real ale as it is usually known) has been our national drink for many hundreds of years. The term 'real ale' was coined by CAMRA in the early 1970s to distinguish the beer people in this country had loved for many years from newer inferior types that were being introduced, mainly by the large national conglomerates.

Real ale is a living beer; the basic ingredients are malt, hops, yeast, water and other natural ingredients. Malt is made from roasting barley and the amount of roasting influences the character and colour of the beer. The brewing process allows the sugar in the malt to ferment with the yeast producing alcohol. The hops provide the bitterness associated with the British style of beer and also add to its character. The beer is racked into casks where more hops or priming sugar may be added and a 'secondary' fermentation takes place; a process essential for the best quality beers. Another name for real ale is 'cask-conditioned' beer.

A substance called finings is added to the final brew which helps clear the beer as it settles in the pub cellar. The skilled publican will be able to judge when the beer is ready to serve in prime condition.

There are literally hundreds of different real beers available in this country so everyone is bound to find a brew they particularly enjoy. The more common ones to be found in Berkshire are listed in the *Breweries* section of this guide.

Good quality beer should not be served too cold or too warm as this impairs the flavour. A recommended cellar temperature is 12–14°C (54–57°F) and a good publican will ensure that the beer does not become too warm before being served.

What is not real ale?

Several new products have been invented in recent times in an attempt to shortcut or simplify the process of keeping and serving beer. All of them have (to date, at least) resulted in a much inferior product. The first of these were poor alternative versions of British beers such as bitter and mild, known as keg beers. These beers are filtered and pasteurised, producing a completely dead, flat liquid which undertakes no secondary fermentation. In order to put some life back into the beer, a canister of carbon dioxide (CO_2) under pressure is plugged into the keg, turning it into a giant aerosol can and making the beer very fizzy.

In the early 1970s, many drinkers objected to these beers, which led to the formation of CAMRA whose aim was to save the traditional style of beer.

Not to be outdone, the brewers turned their attention to faking foreign lagers; aiming them mainly at younger drinkers, using massive advertising campaigns. Initially many lagers were given fake German or Scandinavian names but once this ruse was tumbled many brewers entered into licensing agreements with foreign companies to use their names. Now anything goes, as long as it sounds foreign: American, Australian, Canadian, Dutch, Irish and even that famous beer-producing nation, France, has got in on the act. Look more closely and the vast majority is factory-produced in Britain, using the same keg-processing techniques.

In the last few years a perhaps even less desirable development has taken place with the production of nitro-keg beers. These are similar to keg beers except they use a mixture of carbon dioxide and nitrogen and are usually sold as 'creamflow' or 'smoothflow'. The end result is a less gassy product, but the nitrogen creates tiny bubbles which form a thick creamy head and the beer often takes several minutes to clear. Using incessant advertising the brewers are continually telling us this is what beer is supposed to look like, which is, of course, rubbish. These beers all have one distinctive characteristic in common: they are virtually tasteless. Almost all keg and nitrokeg beers are served chillingly cold to disguise their flavour, or lack of it.

Beer types

There are many types of beer available in this country; the following is an indication of the ones most often to be found. It should be noted that **beer strength** is measured in Alcohol By Volume (ABV), expressed as a percentage, for example 4.3% ABV. This does not mean that the stronger the beer the better; in fact there are many excellent beers available at under 4% ABV.

Bitter is the most common traditional style of British beer. It is lighter in colour than stouts or dark milds but richer than most lagers. A good session bitter (often called 'ordinary bitter') will be between 3.5% and 4% ABV with Special or Best bitter between 4% and 5%. Some bitters are brewed stronger than 5% and often take on a sweeter flavour: they should be treated with respect.

Mild is undoubtedly Britain's most underrated beer. Very popular some years ago, it now seems to suffer an image problem. Most southern milds (there are very few left) are dark in colour and the mildness comes from the fact that they are less hoppy than bitters. An excellent session beer or lunchtime pint. If you are lucky enough to stumble across a pub selling real draught mild, savour a pint immediately.

IPA (India Pale Ale). Originally a strong, clear, hoppy beer brewed to withstand the journey to India for the army based there, many IPAs are now brewed much weaker but can be tasty nonetheless.

Porter and **Stout**. Once the most popular drink in Britain, porters are now hardly to be found except from the occasional microbrewer (local brewer Butts brews an excellent one). They are virtually black in colour from the deep roasted malt and have a wonderful, almost burnt bitterness which lingers. Stouts are the modern version of porter and can be sweet or bitter. Most stouts are, unfortunately, of the keg variety and consequently lack any real depth of flavour. In order to maintain a trendy image, some keg stout manufacturers are now promoting their products in a chillingly cold version; an unforgivable sin for this beer style.

Old ale used to be specially aged but nowadays the name is usually applied to a mid to strong dark winter ale.

Winter ale is invariably strong (at least 4.5%) and because of the high alcohol content it is able to last for several weeks, developing a rich rounded glowing flavour: ideal for keeping out the winter chill. Many winter beers are best served at close to room temperature.

Summer ales are a recent development and are typically golden in colour and moderate in strength. Many use lager hops and are particularly recommended for lager drinkers who would not otherwise dare to sample the delights of proper beer. Can be served slightly colder than most traditional beers.

Seasonal beers. The last few years have seen a massive growth in seasonal beers (in addition to the above) with a whole variety of new beers and ales. One older type is OBJ (O be Joyful) which traditionally was an autumn ale celebrating the harvest home.

Lager is one of the great beer styles of the world. Sadly, much British lager is poor stuff and even if you pay for a strong one, it may well be seriously lacking in flavour. Do not be deceived by the foreign-sounding name: most lager sold in this country is produced by the large conglomerates in factories in Britain.

Barley wine is not a wine at all but a rich, very strong ale usually only served in half-pints (or a nip bottle – one-third pint). At high strength, ale develops a wine-like character; hence the name. This beer should be sipped and only then if not driving.

Methods of serving beer

There are three accepted methods of serving real beer from the cask in England. The first of these employs the use of gravity (shown as Ⓖ in this guide). When the beer is ready, a tap is banged into the end of the cask through a bung hole and the beer pours out naturally once the tap is opened. In many ways this is the best method for serving beer as it does not come into contact with any other apparatus and will therefore be served as the brewer intended. Limitations on space and problems with temperature control mean that few pubs now regularly employ this method of beer dispense but the popularity of mini beer festivals in some pubs often results in a return to serving beer 'straight from the cask'.

The second, and by far most popular, method of serving beer is through a handpump, shown as Ⓗ, or 'beer engine' as it is more properly known. This allows the beer to be kept in a remote, temperature-controlled cellar. As with most serving methods, it is important for the lines (pipes) to be cleaned on a regular basis to ensure that no contamination is caused. The real advantage of handpumps is that a drinker in an unfamiliar pub can usually quickly detect the availability of real beer, although certain breweries and pub chains have been known to use fake handpumps on non-real beers.

The third method involves the use of an electric pump, shown as Ⓔ, which is rare in Berkshire and is mainly likely to be used when the bar is some distance from the cellar.

A recent worrying development in some pubs is the use of swan necks and sparklers on handpumps. The swan neck is a long nozzle which hoops round (like a swan's neck) and down into the bottom of the glass when being filled. This, in itself, is not a major problem, apart from the unnecessary exposure of the nozzle to the air before being dipped into the next pint pulled; however, they are usually associated with the use of a sparkler, a small screw-on device which agitates the beer as it is served, creating lots of foam, resulting in a thick head. The first problem here is that it is difficult to get a full pint of liquid in a glass with such a large head. This may be popular with some landlords but not so with most drinkers. Of even more concern is the effect it has on the beer itself. As explained previously, the less interference to the beer before it gets in the glass the better and the unnecessary agitation to the beer forces the bitterness out of the liquid into the head, making the body of the beer blander, and occasionally metallic-tasting.

These are common in parts of northern England where the locals insist upon a thick head on their beer and the beer is specially brewed to accommodate this. However, traditional southern beers are not intended to be treated in this manner. Just to confuse matters further, some sparklers are added to ordinary-looking handpump nozzles. As in all cases, you are the customer; you are paying for the beer and, above all, you've got to drink it, so have the beer served the way you like. If that means without a sparkler, ask for it to be removed. It only takes a few seconds and a decent publican will willingly oblige.

Once a cask has been tapped, as the beer is removed it is replaced by air (although the cask will contain some natural carbon dioxide (CO_2) caused by the secondary fermentation). Once broached, the beer will remain in prime condition for several days but pubs who serve very little of a particular beer (or have too many beers on at once) can end up selling stale beer. To overcome this, a method of keeping the beer in good condition was introduced by some breweries some years ago, called the cask breather (also known as a demand valve or aspirator). This cannot be detected in the bar as it works by applying carbon dioxide or other gas at about atmospheric pressure into the cask to replace the beer as it is drawn off. Because the beer remaining is not exposed to the air, it remains saleable for longer. This apparatus has been the subject of much controversy amongst beer drinkers, but it is against CAMRA policy to recommend any beers served in this way. It is believed there are more appropriate ways to overcome this problem, such as ordering smaller-sized casks for low turnover beers, or reducing the number of beers stocked at one time. Some genuine beer pubs can easily accommodate eight or nine beers simultaneously, whereas others ought to consider having only one or two beers, which can then be kept in top condition. There is no merit in having a grand selection of beers with many in poor condition.

About CAMRA

CAMRA is the beer lovers' organisation. It was founded in 1972 by a small group of disgruntled beer drinkers who were keen to find out why much of the beer they were drinking had become bland. They discovered that in the 1960s much of the beer production in Britain had become concentrated into a small number of national brewery companies (known as the Big Six) who were intent on pushing standard brands of keg beer, often using the relatively new medium of national television advertising. Epitomising this move was Watney's Red Revolution which became an early target for the fledgling beer-drinkers' organisation. Many years on, Red Barrel is no more (nor indeed is Watney's), but most brewing in Britain is now in the hands of an even smaller number of multi-national companies who are intent upon domination with their latest in fashion beers often aimed at younger drinkers.

Today, CAMRA is needed more than ever and the following are just some of the issues on which we are currently campaigning:

Guest beers A tremendous success was achieved when CAMRA persuaded the government to force large brewery companies to allow guest beers into their pubs. However, much of the impact of this measure has been lost due to the growth of independent pub chains. CAMRA is in discussions with a number of these to ensure a future for many of the excellent beers produced by brewers who do not have the guaranteed outlets offered by the tied house system.

Beer duty The beer duty in Britain is seven times higher than in France, leading to the legal and illegal importation of a massive amount of beer to the detriment of not only brewers but also our pubs. In addition to an overall reduction in beer duty, CAMRA is also pressurising the government to introduce a sliding scale of duty so that many smaller brewers are not penalised for the lack of mass production methods. Similar taxation schemes operate in many other countries.

Licensing laws The 1980s finally saw all-day opening but CAMRA believes that pubs should be allowed to open when they please, subject, of course, to suitable controls to avoid nuisance to local communities.

Full pint The law is an ass; and very confused. You wouldn't be happy to pay for a dozen eggs and only receive eleven, so why pay for a pint of beer and only receive 18 fluid ounces (or less) instead of 20? If you are short-measured, the pub is supposed to top up the glass on request and do so 'with good grace', so politely ask for a top-up.

Beer quality Real beer is wonderful stuff but it does need to be treated properly. Good cellar practice should be second nature to a publican but, sadly, not all seem to follow simple procedures. Many parts of the brewing industry are now addressing the problem, such as the recently launched 'Cask Marque' quality control scheme which employs independent audits to improve beer quality. However, if you are served a pint of something that tastes like vinegar, don't hesitate: ask for it to be changed.

Brewery and pub closures The last few years have seen the loss of two local breweries: Gibbs Mew at Salisbury and the excellent Morrell's of Oxford with two other southern breweries are under serious threat: Courage at Bristol and Morland's of Abingdon. Many of our finest country pubs are also at risk and it is CAMRA's policy to support local breweries and pubs, especially when threatened with closure. Rural pubs are threatened by more stringent drink-and-drive legislation (which we support) and by absence of rural public transport, which we are campaigning to redress. Smaller urban pubs are threatened by the spate of large town centre mega-boozers, taking away their trade. Both are threatened by the accountants employed by many breweries, looking for a fast buck to balance the books.

If all this sounds very serious, that's because real beer lovers take their subject very seriously indeed (and take in a lot of practice!) However, above everything else, being a member of CAMRA is about having fun. If you like meeting people, be they publicans, locals, brewers or fellow beer enthusiasts, then this is the place for you. Branches operate throughout the country and always welcome new people to join in their activities. Throughout the year many beer drinkers flock to CAMRA-organised beer festivals, culminating in the biggest of all, the Great British Beer Festival, held annually in August; which seems to have found a permanent home in London's Olympia. An event not to be missed.

CAMRA in Berkshire

CAMRA in Berkshire is organised into three branches: West Berkshire, Reading & Mid-Berkshire (includes Wokingham and Bracknell) and Slough, Windsor & Maidenhead. Each branch is run independently although joint ventures do take place (such as the production of this guide!) Other activities include regular social events (mostly in pubs), brewery visits, surveying pubs for the national CAMRA *Good Beer Guide* and visiting or helping to run beer festivals. Each branch also produces its own newsletter to look out for while travelling around the county. These are *Ullage* (West Berks), *Thames Valley Drinker* (Reading & Mid-Berks) and *CAMRA Angle* (Slough, Windsor & Maidenhead). Assistance in production and distribution is always most welcome.

In 1995, Reading inaugurated a very successful Beer Festival which has become one of the leading events in the country. It is run annually in late April or early May, currently under canvas in a site at King's Meadow but a suitable indoor venue is being sought.

In association with South Oxfordshire branch, the Reading branch takes the lead in running the 'Festival of Ales', held as part of the popular Woodcote Steam Rally (about six miles north-west of Reading), held in July each year. Workers and drinkers are most welcome to both events. In fact, the local branches are always delighted to welcome new members to any of their activities held throughout the year.

All members receive a monthly newspaper, *What's Brewing*, which lists details of all forthcoming events, and also gives details of who the local branch contacts are. Members also receive a generous discount or free entry to all CAMRA-run events anywhere in the country, plus discounts on publications, like the many local county pub guides and the annual best-selling *Good Beer Guide*.

Contact us

The three branch contacts for Berkshire are:

- *West Berkshire*
  Clive Stevens: (01488) 683398
- *Reading & Mid-Berkshire*
  Janet Blurton: (0118) 961 9140
- *Slough, Windsor & Maidenhead*
  Vic Powell: (01753) 735765

Alternatively, you can contact CAMRA on (01727) 867201 or visit us on the Web at www.camra.org.uk.

The breweries

Large-scale brewing of cask conditioned ale in Berkshire came to an end with the closure of the then Courage-owned ex-Simonds brewery in the centre of Reading in 1980. Its replacement was the massive industrial unit located on the M4 to the south of Reading, created solely for the production of factory-processed beers which deserve no place in a publication dedicated to the discerning drinker.

Excellent beer is produced in Berkshire, however, thanks to a small number of micro breweries and home-brew pubs which have sprung up in recent years. In addition, fine beers from outside the Royal County can be found with the use of this guide, with details of all the main breweries to supply the county's pubs listed below.

In addition to the standard range of beers, many brewers now produce regular seasonal beers, available only at certain times of the year, or beers brewed for special occasions.

Berkshire breweries and brew-pubs

Butts Brewery

Northfield Farm, Wantage Road, Great Shefford, near Hungerford

Berkshire is a richer county since the creation of Butts brewery in converted farm buildings in autumn 1994. The beer range has gradually increased as trade has expanded to over 80 pubs, many of which are in Berkshire. The beers are extremely flavoursome (particularly for their gravity) and should be tried on every occasion they are encountered. Blackguard is an excellent porter. Barbus Barbus is Latin for the barbel fish.

- ❑ Jester (ABV 3.5%)
- ❑ Bitter (ABV 4%)
- ❑ Blackguard (ABV 4.5%)
- ❑ Barbus Barbus (ABV 4.6%)

Brewery Tap brew-pub

Castle Street, Reading

Operated by the Tudor brewing company, this brew-pub opened in early 1999 in the old Courage social club with assistance from Kent brewers Shepherd Neame. Beer range will increase as the operation becomes more established.

- ❑ Brewer's Choice Red (ABV 4.3%)
- ❑ Brewer's Choice Green (ABV 3.9%)

Flyer & Firkin brew-pub

54 Blagrave Street, Reading

Original idea of Firkin home brew-pubs created by David Bruce in 1979. Now in the ownership of Allied-Domecq but are likely to become a Whitbread brand if the latter succeed in their bid for Allied's pubs. The 'Flyer' and the 'Fort' in Windsor brew some of their own beer but other Firkin pubs in the county do not. It is believed that currently only Flyer is brewed at Reading with the other beers coming from other Firkin breweries.

- ❑ Firkin Best (ABV 3.8%)
- ❑ Flyer (ABV 4.3%)
- ❑ Dogbolter (ABV 5.6%)

Fort & Firkin brew-pub
The Promenade, Windsor
Like the Reading brewery, it is likely that not all the following are brewed in Windsor.
- ❑ Royale (ABV 3.4%)
- ❑ Best (ABV 3.8%)
- ❑ Fort Ale (ABV 4.3%)
- ❑ Dogbolter (ABV 5.6%)
- ❑ Porter (ABV 4.6%)

Reading Lion Brewery
The Hop Leaf, 163–165 Southampton Street, Reading
Small satellite brewery owned by the Hop Back brewery of Salisbury, from where most of the beers are supplied. Home-brewed beers are not always available but are certainly worth sampling when they are.

West Berkshire Brewery
Pot Kiln Lane, Frilsham, Yattendon
An excellent micro brewery located in an old brick works in grounds behind the Pot Kiln pub, set up in September 1995. The beers quickly established a reputation for quality, and consequently brewing capacity has been increased to cope with demand. Occasional seasonal and special brews are produced.
- ❑ Skiff (ABV 3.6%)
- ❑ Magg's Magnificent Mild (ABV 3.8%)
- ❑ Good Old Boy (ABV 4%)
- ❑ Dr Hexter's Wedding Ale (ABV 4.1%)
- ❑ Graft Bitter (ABV 4.3%)
- ❑ Dr Hexter's Healer (ABV 5%)
- ❑ Goldstar (ABV 5%)

In addition:

Original Brewing Company brew-pub
Hollywood Bowl, The Point, Skimpedhill Lane, Bracknell
Owned by Bass, this small brewery produces a range of its own beers (rather noisily) next to the bowling alley in Bracknell. The beers are stored in cellar tanks under carbon dioxide gas and, therefore, cannot be classified as real ale.

Breweries with pubs in Berkshire

Independent breweries

Arkell's Brewery
Kingsdown, Swindon, Wilts
Established 1843. Almost 100 tied houses mostly based close to the brewery. Few are in Berkshire, although one is a real outpost at Woodside near Ascot. Also available in free houses (the brewery has about 200 free trade accounts). Seasonal beers also produced.
- ❑ 2B (or BB) (ABV 3.2%)
- ❑ 3B (or BBB) (ABV 4%)
- ❑ Kingsdown Ale (ABV 5%)

Badger Brewery (Hall & Woodhouse)
Blandford St Mary, Dorset
Established 1777. Recently renamed to its popular name from the more formal Hall & Woodhouse, the brewers of Badger beer are another local brewery gradually expanding beyond their traditional west country homeland. Golden Champion is a recent addition following the success of the stronger bottled version.
- ❑ IPA (ABV 3.6%)
- ❑ Dorset Best (ABV 4.1%)
- ❑ Tanglefoot (ABV 5.1%)
- ❑ Golden Champion (ABV 4.6%)

W. H. Brakspear & Sons
Henley Brewery, New Street, Henley-on-Thames, Oxon
Established 1779. Just a stone's throw across the Thames from Berkshire, this excellent brewery is well represented in the county with a number of tied houses providing a virtual guarantee of a good pint. Interesting range of seasonal beers. The company has recently ventured into producing bottle-conditioned beers including an excellent bottled version of Bluebird (ABV 4.2%). Pins of all the company's draught beers are available from the brewery shop (give 48 hours notice) in addition to decanted draught bitter.

- XXX Mild (ABV 3%)
- Bitter (often referred to as 'ordinary') (ABV 3.4%)
- Special Bitter (ABV 4.3%)
- XXXX Old Ale (ABV 4.3%)
- Coniston Bluebird (contract brewed) (ABV 3.6%)
- The Abroad Cooper (for Hogshead chain) (ABV 5.1%)

Harvey & Son
Bridge Wharf Brewery, Cliffe High Street, Lewes, East Sussex
Established in the 18th century. A fairly recent but welcomed addition to the Berkshire pub scene as Harvey's is gradually branching out from its homeland near the south coast. One of the pioneers of seasonal beers, which are always worth a try for a different pint.

- Sussex XX Mild Ale (ABV 3%)
- Sussex Pale Ale (ABV 3.5%)
- Sussex Best Bitter (ABV 4%)
- Armada Ale (ABV 4.5%)
- Old Ale (ABV 4.3%) (available Oct–May)

Fuller, Smith & Turner
Griffin Brewery, Chiswick Lane South, Chiswick W4
Established 1845. Famous west London brewers, Fuller's have won numerous awards for their beers at CAMRA festivals with 'Pride' becoming a standard

guest beer in the repertoire of many pub chains. Regular seasonal beers.

- ❑ Chiswick Bitter (ABV 3.5%)
- ❑ London Pride (ABV 4.1%)
- ❑ ESB (Extra Special Bitter) (ABV 5.5%)

George Gale & Co.
The Brewery, Horndean, Hants
Established 1847. The producers of Gale's Ales have been gradually expanding their range of beers following an expansion of brewing capacity a few years ago. The very popular HSB should not overshadow the other very good Hampshire beers. Take care with the bottle-conditioned Prize Old Ale which has an ABV of 9%.

- ❑ Butser Bitter (ABV 3.4%)
- ❑ GB (Gale's Bitter) (ABV 4%)
- ❑ HSB (Horndean Special Bitter) (ABV 4.8%)
- ❑ Festival Mild (ABV 4.8%)

Greene King
Westgate Brewery, Westgate Street, Bury St Edmunds, Suffolk
Established 1799. Since its abortive attempt to take over Morland's of Abingdon in 1991, the large East Anglia brewer has been rapidly expanding its estate including several pubs in Berkshire. The beer range is not the most inspired but a relatively new beer, Triumph Bitter, shows that the brewery has not forgotten how to produce good quality beers. Also, interesting seasonal brews.

- ❑ Dark (ABV 3%)
- ❑ Martha Greene Bitter (ABV 3.1%)
- ❑ IPA (India Pale Ale) (ABV 3.6%)
- ❑ Triumph Bitter (ABV 4.3%)
- ❑ Abbot Ale (ABV 5%)

Hop Back Brewery
Batten Road, Downton, Salisbury, Wilts
Established 1987. This small brewery has won deserved acclaim since its founding as a brew-pub in Salisbury. All the beers are superb but Summer Lightning has reached almost cult status.

- ❑ GFB (ABV 3.5%)
- ❑ Best Bitter (ABV 4.0%)
- ❑ Entire Stout (ABV 4.5%)
- ❑ Thunderstorm (ABV 5%)
- ❑ Summer Lightning (ABV 5%)

Marston, Thompson & Evershed
Shobnall Road, Burton-on-Trent, Staffs
Following a fierce battle, Marston's were taken over by Wolverhampton & Dudley in early 1999, ironically at about the time Pedigree became Britain's best-selling cask conditioned ale. Brewing looks safe at Marston's brewery, at least for the time being, although its long-term survival cannot be guaranteed. Pedigree is widely available as a guest beer in many of Berkshire's pubs. Following the take-over, the few Marston's tied houses in the county are likely in future to receive their beers from Greene King.

- ❑ Bitter (ABV 3.8%)
- ❑ Pedigree (ABV 4.5%)
- ❑ Owd Rodger (ABV 7.6%)

Morland

The Brewery, Ock Street, Abingdon, Oxon

Established 1711. The most widely represented independent brewer in Berkshire, having fought off a hostile take-over attempt in 1991 from Greene King, have, unbelieveably, entered into discussions with the East Anglian company which could well yet see the take-over and closure of the Abingdon brewery. A number of disastrous moves have led to this state of affairs, not least Morland's costly take-over and closure of Ruddles' famous Rutland brewery in 1997.

The only Morland beer likely to survive if the take-over goes ahead is Old Speckled Hen, although what will happen to the Ruddles name is anybody's guess. Independent IPA, brewed to celebrate the successful defence against Greene King, is likely to disappear sooner rather than later.

- ❑ Independent IPA (ABV 3.4%)
- ❑ Original Bitter (ABV 3.7%)
- ❑ Tanner's Jack (ABV 4.4%)
- ❑ Old Speckled Hen (ABV 5.2%)
- ❑ Ruddles Best Bitter (ABV 3.7%)
- ❑ Ruddles County (ABV 4.9%)

Ushers

The Brewery, Fore Street, Trowbridge, Wilts

Established 1824. Yet another local brewery to increase its establishment of houses in Berkshire in recent years.

A management buy-out from Courage in 1991 saw Usher's regain its independence, lost in 1960 when it became part of the dreaded Watney's red revolution. Since then, the company has acquired a number of pubs in the county. Some interesting seasonal ales.

- ❑ Best Bitter (ABV 3.8%)
- ❑ Founders Ale (ABV 4.5%)

Wadworth & Co.

Northgate Brewery, Devizes, Wilts

Established 1885. Another reliable independent brewer with a sprinkling of tied houses throughout the county. Their most famous beer, 6X, is widely available as a guest beer and in free houses. In an interesting variation on the seasonal beers theme, the company is now producing a number of single-variety hop beers.

- ❑ Henry's Original IPA (ABV 3.8%)
- ❑ 6X (ABV 4.3%)
- ❑ Farmer's Glory (ABV 4.5%)

Wychwood Brewery Co.

The Crofts, Corn Street, Witney, Oxon

Established 1983. Another successful 'new' brewery company that has expanded to run over thirty 'Hobgoblin' pubs, only a small number of which reside in Berkshire. Dog's Bollocks has recently been switched from regular production to be one of a number of seasonal beers.

- ❑ Shires XXX (ABV 3.7%)
- ❑ Special (ABV 4.2%)
- ❑ The Dog's Bollocks (ABV 5.2%)

National breweries

Bass Brewers Ltd

137 High Street, Burton-on-Trent, Staffs

Until recently Britain's largest brewer and producer of the country's best selling cask conditioned beer, Draught Bass, the company has really lost its way as far as beer drinkers are concerned. 'Our Finest Beer' was the slogan Bass proudly attributed to its flagship brand and, although still widely available in Berkshire, the company seem far more interested in promoting their factory processed beers and lagers. The closure of a number of breweries in recent years has led to the loss of several regional ales.

- Draught Bass (ABV 4.4%)
- Worthington Best Bitter (ABV 3.6%)
- Hancock's HB (ABV 3.6%)

Carlsberg-Tetley Brewing Ltd

Burton-on-Trent, Staffs

Formed by the merger of Allied Breweries with Danish company Carlsberg in 1992, this is now a brewery company with no pubs as these are now run by Allied-Domecq (including the Firkin brew-pubs in Reading and Windsor) but the whole estate is subject to interest by Whitbread. Once widely available in Berkshire, only the Leeds-brewed Tetley bitter is now common although Ind Coope Burton Ale (CAMRA's champion beer of Britain in 1990) can occasionally be found.

- Tetley Bitter (ABV 3.7%)
- Ind Coope Burton Ale (ABV 4.8%)

Scottish Courage Ltd

111 Holyrood Road, Edinburgh, Lothian

Formed in 1995 by the takeover of Courage by Scottish & Newcastle Breweries to become Britain's largest brewing company. Courage Best and Directors come from the old George's brewery in Bristol but in 1999 the company announced its proposed closure, transferring them to Tadcaster, North Yorkshire.

- Courage Best (ABV 4%)
- Courage Directors (ABV 4.8%)
- Theakston Best (ABV 3.8%)
- Theakston XB (ABV 4.6%)

Whitbread plc

Porter Tun House, Capability Green, Luton, Beds

Another large brewery company to close many local breweries (not least, the excellent Wethered's of Marlow in 1988), the company now puts most of its faith for cask beer sales in the Boddington brand name. Following the closure of the Cheltenham brewery in 1998, other brands were transferred to the Manchester brewery. As this guide was in preparation, Whitbread were strongly rumoured to be seeking to pull out of brewing completely (after over 250 years) in order to concentrate on their pub owning and numerous other business activities.

- Boddingtons Bitter (ABV 3.8%)
- Flowers IPA (ABV 3.6%)
- Flower's Original (ABV 4.4%)
- Trophy Bitter (ABV 3.8%)
- Whitbread Best (ABV 3.6%)

Noted micros

Hogs Back Brewery

The Street, Tongham, Surrey

Established in an eighteenth century farm building in 1992, this brewery has gone from strength to strength and now produces some 20 beers over the course of a year. The prize winning TEA is widely available in the free trade. The brewery shop offers polypins and smaller take-away containers for decanted real beer.

- Hair of the Hog (ABV 3.5%)
- TEA (Traditional English Ale) (ABV 4.2%)
- Hop Garden Gold (ABV 4.6%)
- Rip Snorter (ABV 5%)

Rebellion Beer Company

Marlow, Bucks

Established in 1993 by two local old school friends and restored Marlow's brewing tradition, shamefully removed with the closure of Wethered's brewery by Whitbread five years earlier. The beers regularly crop up as guests or in free houses and are fully recommended as excellent ales. A number of seasonal ales have recently been introduced.

- IPA (ABV 3.7%)
- Smuggler (ABV 4.1%)
- Blonde Bombshell (ABV 4.3%)
- Mutiny (ABV 4.5%)

Clubs

Twenty years ago, it was almost impossible to find a private members' club, whether one of the national chains organised by the CIU and the Conservatives, or those associated with places of work, serving real ale. Fortunately, this position has changed over the years and some clubs, such as the excellent Hungerford Club, have attained an entry in the Good Beer Guide (GBG). This club admits CAMRA members and members of the general public bearing a copy of the GBG and is listed in the directory section of this guide. Others believed to sell real ale but where you will probably need to be a member to gain entry include:

- Maidenhead, Ivy Leaf Club, Holmanleaze.
- Maidenhead Conservative Club, York Road.
- Newbury, Royal British Legion Club, Pelican Lane.
- Pangbourne, Working Man's Club.
- Reading, Balfour Club, Eldon Square.
- Reading Post Office Club, Richfield Avenue.
- Wargrave, Working Men's Club, Church Street.
- Windsor, Royal Antediluvian Order of Buffaloes Club.

We should be pleased to hear from readers with any further information in this area.

Opening hours

For most of the twentieth century the opening times of our pubs were restricted by emergency legislation introduced during the First World War to protect output from munitions factories. It was seventy years after the cessation of hostilities before the government realised we had sufficient Sopwith Camels, and in 1988 afternoon drinking was reintroduced into England. Another seven years passed before full-day opening was extended to Sundays. Following the national jamboree of the millennium New Year's Eve celebrations, further liberalisation of the licensing laws is promised. In addition to additional potential opening hours, the likely outcome is far greater flexibility in pub opening. The opening hours listed in this publication should, therefore, be treated as a guide only and confirmation should be sought if an important pub visit is planned.

The pub – our heritage

As can be seen throughout the pages of this guide, Berkshire has dozens of wonderful historic pubs, many of them dating back several centuries. The public house is intertwined with British society history: our heritage.

But there has been a dramatic change in pub ownership in the last ten years with the emergence of large pub owning groups. In many cases the pub is seen as a commodity which must maximise profits and may be bought and sold on a whim, often in job-lots of hundreds. It is an incredible fact that the biggest owner of pubs in Britain is a Japanese bank!

Each year hundreds of pubs are closed, demolished or otherwise ruined. Those that survive are often spoilt; lovely old interiors ripped out in the cause of 'modernisation'.

Plans to gut the Cross Keys at Pangbourne have recently been turned down by the local planning committee following objections by villagers and the Reading CAMRA branch.

In order to help protect old pubs which remain intact or little altered, CAMRA has created a national inventory of heritage pubs. Berkshire has two entries: the Bell at Aldworth and the Pot Kiln at Frilsham.

Within a few weeks of each other in spring 1999, two pubs in our county were badly damaged by fire. While the lovely old thatched Greyhound at Tidmarsh is well on the way to being restored, the future of the Three Jays at Sunninghill is less certain.

But the main culprits destroying pubs are the businesses that do not see a pub as a piece of history but as an investment upon which optimum profit must be gained or the asset is liquefied. Over thirty pubs listed in the last edition of this guide ten years ago no longer trade. Granted, not all were thatched taverns or old coaching inns but the little Victorian street-corner local is just as much a part of our heritage.

One of CAMRA's major campaigns over the years has been pub preservation and each branch has a Pub Preservation Officer. If you hear about a pub being under threat of closure or being ruined, give your local branch a ring. You do not have to be a member, and you will get advice and support to help save a piece of history.

It is unlikely that in a hundred years time a pressure group will be formed to save twentieth-century supermarkets or car parks. Pubs are important; once they're gone, they're gone for good.

Public transport

Being a responsible organisation, CAMRA discourages drinking and driving, and supports public transport, especially its extension into rural areas. Berkshire is a mixture of large towns (which are well served) and rural areas (which are less so) and most local CAMRA events are based at venues easily accessible by public transport. Recommended pubs listed in the guide within half a mile of a railway station receive a special symbol (⇌).

To support some of our vulnerable country pubs, we also undertake car sharing visits (boring for the driver who drinks very expensive orange juice), or coach trips with pick-up points in main towns.

If you cannot join us but would like to plan a visit to some of the delightful pubs to be found in this guide, the telephone numbers of the main public transport providers in the county are listed below.

Buses

The main bus companies in Berkshire are:

- Reading Buses (0118) 959 4000
- Newbury Buses (01635) 40743
- Beeline, Bracknell (01344) 424938
- Beeline, Slough (01753) 524144

Trains

The main train operators in the county are:

- First Great Western
- South West Trains
- Thames Trains
- Virgin Trains

Timetable enquiries should be made on the national enquiry number: 0345 484950

Minicom 0845 605 0600

Ten years in the life of CAMRA in Berkshire

John Dearing
Chairman of the Reading and Mid-Berkshire Branch

This Guide is being published on the tenth anniversary of the last Berkshire Guide. It is a sobering thought (or maybe one likely to drive one to drink) that in the previous fifteen years of CAMRA activity in the county five guides were produced including the last one. This does not mean that CAMRA in Berkshire has been inactive. In 1995, the Reading Branch inaugurated a very successful Beer Festival which has become established as one of the leading events in the country, popular with beer-tickers and normal people alike. The first of these highlighted the absence of a real ale brewery in the county and behold, within the next year or so we had four, although one of these, Greenwood's of Wokingham, has sadly not lasted the pace, in spite of the very high reputation of its beers. Butts, West Berkshire and Reading Lion brewery are also greatly admired, and to these must be added the two brewing Firkins at Windsor and Reading, Bass's Original Brewing Co. in Bracknell's Hollywood Bowl and the most recent arrival, Tudor Brewing Co. which has brought brewing in Reading back to its historical origins in Castle Street.

The Berkshire and Oxfordshire branches joined together to campaign against the take-over of Morland's brewery by Greene King, which would have led to the closure of Berkshire's oldest surviving brewery, which has been exiled to Oxfordshire since 1974. With the news that Morland have now entered into voluntary discussions with Greene King which may lead to their take-over, we must wonder why we bothered.

The past ten years have also seen changes in the availability of real ale, which could hardly have been predicted back in 1989. Reading in particular has become a sort of Newcastle of the south with teeny-boppers trooping from pub to pub in the town's new 'Beer Mile'. Surprisingly, nearly all of the fifteen or so new pubs which have opened up in the town in recent years serve real ale, some of it of a high quality. New pubs have also sprung up in most of the other major centres, including Newbury, Slough and Maidenhead, while the growth of the Hobgoblin chain has revitalised a number of tired old pubs. However, all this has not been without its price. The new pubs have been largely situated in town centres and they have tended to take trade away from many of the smaller locals, some of which have found it impossible to survive. These include my old local, the Cambridge Arms, which declined rapidly in the space of five years from being one of Morland's most popular pubs to not much better than a doss-house. The determination of the bigger brewers to push nitro-keg products has also meant that some publicans have found it difficult to maintain real ale sales with the inevitable result of removed or disused handpumps. Rumour has it that a trend is starting back towards smaller local pubs – well, life does tend to go in cycles and we would certainly welcome it. The very fact that the Reading Branch elected one relatively small town pub as its Pub of the Year for 1998, with another as runner-up, shows where our hearts lie. In the country, too, the pub is under threat and CAMRA at its most recent conference undertook to campaign vigorously for the rural pub, in particular by encouraging and publicising transport links.

The position of the leading groups in the industry has also changed. Now the Big Three rather than the Big Six, they still control the market to a very large degree, although they no longer own as many pubs as they used to. Locally, the most obvious evidence of this is the disappearance of that much-overworked rooster, the Courage cockerel, from our pub signs with large swathes of former Courage pubs bought up by Morland's, Greene King (direct or via Magic Pubs) and others. In some cases the extension of choice was somewhat illusory since Morland's, for instance, have merited the award of the decade for asset-stripping by closing three of the pubs they acquired in Reading.

The big brewers' commitment to real ale varies. Whitbread has closed much of its brewing capacity and its recent moves of Allied-Domecq are likely to require the hiving off of its remaining breweries, although it will no doubt wish to continue supply arrangements for Boddingtons as its national brand. It has also made up for the shortfall in its own production by supplying other brewers' beer in particular through its Hogshead chain and no doubt this process will continue as it becomes the largest non-brewing pub group. Scottish Courage likewise appears to regard real ale as a valuable part of their portfolio, even though we may think much of it disappointingly bland. Nevertheless, there are rumours that the old George's brewery in Bristol, where Courage Best and Directors is now brewed, may be under threat of closure. The greatest enigma is Bass, once proud of brewing more real ale than anybody else but now pushing Caffreys Nitro-keg at the expense of their former flagship ale brand, Draught Bass. A recent visit to the Bass-owned Harvester in Reading revealed not one drop of Bass-brewed real ale, but plenty of Carling, Tennents and Caffreys, keg Worthington, alleviated fortunately by a bank of four handpumps each dispensing Fuller's London Pride.

What this all adds up to is that CAMRA still has a job to do. We cannot afford to sit back and relax in complacency – eternal vigilance or else! If you enjoy real ale (and if you don't why did you buy this book?) and wish to continue to enjoy it, the safest way of pursuing your desire is to make your contribution by joining CAMRA, adding your voice to the 50,000 plus who already support the campaign, and becoming a more informed drinker through reading our excellent monthly newspaper, *What's Brewing*. Fill in the form near the back of this book and we shall look forward to welcoming you as a member.

Pub listings

Comments/updates

We have tried to ensure that the information in this guide is as accurate as possible, but changes are inevitable. If you have any comments on the entries, if you discover any changes to the pubs listed, or if you would like to receive free updates, please e-mail us at:

berkshire.pubs@virgin.net

Aldermaston D4

Dominated by the atomic research establishment and famed for its CND marches. There was once a brewery at the rear of the Hind's Head. Aldermaston Wharf, once home to Strange's brewery, and the station are some distance from the village.

Butt Inn

Station Road (A340)
☎ (0118) 971 2129
12-2.30, 6-11; 12-5, 7-10.30 (Sun)
Wadworth 6X; Flowers Original; Boddingtons Bitter Ⓗ
Large open aspect pub close to Kennet & Avon canal. Popular with boaters and ramblers. Open all day during summer. Meals served every lunchtime and evening (except Mon eve). Named after the archery butts, formerly in the field opposite. *Recommended.*
P

Hinds Head

Wasing Lane
☎ (0118) 971 2194
11-2.30, 5 (6 Sat)-11; 12-3, 7-10.30 (Sun)
Fuller's London Pride; Gales GB, HSB, Butser Ⓗ
Attractive, comfortable village inn providing accommodation. Food served every lunchtime and evening. Popular with business people at lunchtimes and locals in the evening. *Recommended.*
Q P

Aldworth D2

Attractive little village (formerly known as Elleorde or Old Town) near the eastern end of the Ridgeway path – where it joins the prehistoric Icknield Way, which ran from Salisbury Plain to The Wash. The village church has huge stone effigies (known locally as The Giants) of the medieval De La Beche family; and there is a yew tree which is reputed to be over 1,000 years old. The old village well used to lift water 372 feet – one of the deepest in England.

Bell Inn

(village centre, off B4009)
☎ (01635) 578272
11-3, 6-11; closed Mon except Bank Hols; 12-3, 7-10.30 (Sun)
West Berkshire Magg's Magnificent Mild, Old Tyler; Arkell's 3B, Kingsdown Ⓗ
Traditional country pub of exceptional historic interest located high in the Berkshire downs. In the same family for many generations. The beer is cheap and always in excellent condition. Likewise, the food (rolls and salad in summer; home-made soup in winter) is cheap and delicious. 'Old Tyler' is Good Old Boy. *Recommended.*
Q P

Four Points

Haw Lane (B4009)
☎ (01635) 578367
11-3, 5.30-11; 11-11 (Sat); 12-10.30 (Sun)
Brakspear Bitter; Wadworth 6X Ⓗ
Small freehouse (despite the Morland's signage) named after road junction to the south of the village. Most frequented by locals but separate eating area attracts diners. Small car park. Food available 12–2 (3 Sat, Sun) and 6.45–9.45 (Mon–Sat).

Arborfield F3

Bramshill Hunt

Bramshill Close (A327)
☎ (0118) 976 0850
12-3.30, 6-11; 12-11 (Wed, Fri, Sun)
Ruddles Best, County Ⓗ
Pub with smoky lounge and pool room next to army base. Very reasonably priced food.

Bull

Swallowfield Road (A327)
☎ (0118) 976 0204
11-3, 6-11; 11-11 (Sat); 12-3, 7-10.30 (Sun)
Courage Best; Draught Bass; Young's Special Ⓗ
Unpretentious 16th-century pub on Arborfield Cross, once briefly visited by Queen Victoria.

The two bars are now interconnected but otherwise mostly unspoilt. Large garden with children's play area. Food available 12–1.45 and 6–8.45. *Recommended.*
❀◐◑P

Swan
Eversley Road (A327)
☎ (0118) 976 0475
11-11; 12-10.30 (Sun)
Draught **Bass**; **Courage Best**, Directors; guest beer Ⓗ
Beamed 'olde worlde' drinking area with two barely separated rooms, another upstairs and a large function room. Guest beer changes regularly. Average priced food menu (food at all times). Car park small and awkward.

Ascot H3

Famous for its racecourse and the annual Royal meeting when thousands fill the town in a mad rush to lose their money on the horses! Most of the pubs are away from the trackside in either North or South Ascot.

At the Station
Station Hill (A330)
☎ (01344) 878100
11-11; 12-10.30 (Sun)
Courage Best; **Greene King** Abbot Ⓗ
Continental style café bar next to the railway station which fronts a popular Jazz and Blues club. Opens from 10 for food and beverages. Previously the Station Hotel.

Cranbourne Tower
112 Fernbank Road, North Ascot (off A329)
☎ (01344) 882150
11-11; 12-10.30 (Sun)
Courage Best; **Theakston** XB; **Wadworth** 6X Ⓗ
Large pub with two bar areas. Typical ex-Big Six corporate bar furniture. Sporting (especially golf) bric-a-brac. *Recommended.*
❀◐◑P

Gold Cup
102 Fernbank Road, North Ascot (off A329)
☎ (01344) 882498
11-3, 5.30-11; 12-3, 5.30-10.30 (Sun)
Morland Original, **Tanners** Jack; **Ruddles** Best Ⓗ
Comfortable but unpretentious beer drinkers' pub, popular with locals. Lounge bar at the front and smaller saloon bar at the rear. Garden adjacent to car park. Named after the famous race at Ascot, first run in 1807.

Royal Hunt
117 New Road, North Ascot
☎ (01344) 882723
1-11; 11-11 (Sat); 12-10.30 (Sun)
Morland Original; **Ruddles** Best, County Ⓗ
Backstreet 17th-century pub, notable because it has not been 'improved'. Retains comfortable real pub feel. Large selection of whiskies. Piano. Separate games bar. Note 1 pm opening Mon–Fri. *Recommended.*
❀♣P

Royal Hunt, Ascot

Stag

63 High Street (A329)
☎ (01344) 621622
11.30-3, 5.30-11; 11-10 (Sat); 12-3, 7-10.30 (Sun)
Greene King IPA, Abbot Ale Ⓗ
Now a one-bar pub with a small area set aside for eating. Stable (genuine) bar and courtyard at rear for race day crowds. Lunch until 2.30, evening food 5.30–9.30 (not Sun). *Recommended.*

Swinley

29 Brockenhurst Road (A330), South Ascot
☎ (01344) 621743
11-11; 12-10.30 (Sun)
Morland Independent IPA, Original; Ruddles County Ⓗ
Street corner local which is larger inside than appears from the outside. Local pictures displayed by long-standing landlady. Renamed from the Railway Arms. Small garden.

Thatched Tavern

Cheapside Road (off B383)
☎ (01344) 620874/623043
11-3, 6-11; 11-11 (Sat); 12-10.30 (Sun)
Fuller's London Pride; Greene King Abbot; Brakspear Bitter Ⓗ
Sixteenth-century pub with flagstone floor and low beams in up-market district. Business lunches a speciality. Restaurant can get very busy and booking is recommended. Prices reflect the district.

Wells

London Road (A329)
☎ (01344) 622757
11-11; 12-10.30 (Sun)
Morland Original, Old Speckled Hen; Ruddles County Ⓗ
Large roadside pub on the eastern extremities of Ascot, given a new lease of life when acquired by Morland from Courage a few years ago. The unusual name derives from the 18th-century Chalybeate Springs which were capped to accommodate the building of the pub in 1880. Separate family room and outdoor children's play area. *Recommended.*
P

Ashmore Green C3

Sun in the Wood

Stoney Lane
☎ (01635) 42377
12-2.30, 6-11; 12-3, 6-11 (Sat); 12-4, 7-10.30 (Sun); closed Mon
Wadworth IPA, 6X; guest beer Ⓗ
Large comfortable country pub with restaurant. Good sized garden includes children's play area. Lunches every day. Eve meals Tue–Sat. *Recommended.*
Q P

Aston G1

Flower Pot

Ferry Lane (off A4130)
☎ (01491) 574721
11-3, 6-11; 12-2.30, 7-10.30 (Sun)
Brakspear Mild, Bitter, Special, seasonal beers Ⓗ
Imposing two-bar hotel with its own Thames landing stage. Wooden floor in public bar frequented by friendly locals. Smart lounge and dining area. Interesting stuffed fish collection. A real gem. No evening meals Sun eve in winter. *Recommended.*
Q P

'There is nothing which has yet been contrived by man, by which so much happiness is produced as by a good tavern or inn'

Dr Samuel Johnson (1709–1784)

Bagnor C3

The village is home to a very successful little theatre in the converted watermill.

Blackbird

(OS 453692)
☎ (01635) 40638
11.30-3, 6-11; 12-3, 7-10.30 (Sun)
Butts Barbus Barbus; **Brakspear** Bitter; **Ushers** Best Ⓗ
A really out-of-the-way picturesque village pub, located at the confluence of the Winterbourne and Lambourn rivers. The long single bar with partitioned restaurant offers a good choice of beers and wines, and a sophisticated menu, no doubt influenced by the nearby Watermill Theatre. *Recommended.*
⌂Q❀◐◑⛫P

Barkham F3

Mentioned in the Domesday Book as being in the Charlton Hundred within the Forest of Windsor. The small village lies on one of the straight rides that criss-crossed the forest.

Bull

Barkham Road (B3349)
☎ (0118) 976 0324
11-11; 12-10.30 (Sun)
Theakston XB; **Courage** Best; guest beers Ⓗ
Grade II listed pub, parts of which date from the mid-1700s. One large bar divided into distinct areas retaining some of its original character including an inglenook fireplace. Separate restaurant in the old smithy with different menu lunch and evenings. Imaginative but pricey guest beers. TV and music. No mobile phones! Food served 12–2, 7–9 every day (booking advised). *Recommended.*
❀◐◑P

Beech Hill E4

Old Elm Tree

Beech Hill Road
☎ (0118) 988 3505
12-2.30, 5-11; 12-2.30, 5-10.30 (Sun)
Adnams Bitter; **Marston's** Bitter, Pedigree; **Fuller's** London Pride Ⓗ
Two contrasting rooms and a restaurant. Easygoing pub atmosphere and soft muzak. There is speculation over the future of this pub. No food Sun eve. *Recommended.*
◐◑⊟P

Beedon C2

Coach & Horses

Oxford Road, World's End
☎ (01635) 248743
12-2.30, 6-11; 12-11 (Sat); 12-10.30 (Sun)
Morland Original Ⓗ
Traditional two-bar village local. Larger public bar to right of entrance porch, quieter lounge to left where food is served. Smoking strongly discouraged in eating area. Occasional guest beer. *Recommended.*
⌂Q❀◐◑⊟♣P

Langley Hall

Oxford Road, World's End
☎ (01635) 248332
12-3, 5.30 (6 Sat)-11; 12-3, 6.30-10.30 (Sun)
West Berkshire Good Old Boy; **Flowers** Original Ⓗ
Public house which has gone through several changes of name and image over the last few years. It has now returned to being a pleasant, large pub serving a local real ale and home cooking: some meals with a South African flavour. *Recommended.*
⌂❀◐◑♿♣P

Jack O'Newbury, Binfield

Beenham D3

Six Bells
(off A4)
☎ (0118) 971 3368
12-3, 6-11; 12-4, 7-10.30 (Sun)
Brakspear Bitter; **Flowers** IPA; **Rebellion** IPA; **Slater's** Premium Ⓗ
Comfortable two-bar village pub. Meals served every lunch and evening. Accommodation (four rooms). *Recommended.*

Stocks Inn
(near Webbs Lane, off A4)
☎ (0118) 971 3127
12-3 (Sat only), 7-11; 12-3, 7-10.30 (Sun)
Shepherd Neame Spitfire; **Charles Wells** Bombardier; **Hook Norton** Best; **Archers** Village; guest beer Ⓗ
Comfortable friendly village pub of some character. Excellent Sunday roasts: no other hot meals served. Named after the well-known punishment method, once situated nearby. *Recommended.*
Q P

Winning Hand
Bath Road (A4)
☎ (0118) 930 2472
12-2.30, 6-11; 12-2.30, 6.30-11 (Sat); 12-2.20, 7-10.30 (Sun)
Brakspear Bitter; **Marstons** Pedigree Ⓗ
Cosy roadside pub-cum-restaurant with B&B accommodation, outside main village. Named after painting found by present owner when moving in during late 1980s.

Binfield G3

Virtually swallowed up by Bracknell but still retaining something of its village feel. It was once the home of the poet Alexander Pope (1688–1744).

Jack o' Newbury
Terrace Road North (B3018)
☎ (01344) 454881
12-3, 5.30-11; 12-3, 7-10.30 (Sun)
Brakspear Bitter, Special Bitter; **Rebellion** IPA; **Badger** Tanglefoot, Dorset Best Ⓗ
Cosy pub with horseshoe-shaped bar area whose walls are covered in brasses and other paraphernalia including a display of guns. Named after 16th-century merchant who aided Henry VIII in his battle against Scots at Flodden Field in 1513. More recently used as a staging post for prisoners in transit from London to Reading Gaol. Complete range of beers not always available.

see page 126

Roebuck
St Marks Road (near A329)
☎ (01344) 423232
11-11; 12-10.30 (Sun)
Morland Original, Old Speckled Hen; **Ruddles** Best; **Marston's** Pedigree Ⓗ
Small and popular locals' pub which offers a very friendly welcome to the casual visitor. Basic range of food available most times except Sunday evening.

Royal Standard
Forest Road
☎ (01344) 423478
11-11; 12-10.30 (Sun)
Morland Independent IPA, Original; **Flowers** Original Ⓗ
The whole front of the pub is taken up by a basic public bar with bare wooden tables, TV and bar billiards. Popular with young drinkers in the evening and can get smoky. The large comfortable lounge is wood-panelled throughout and is accessed via the car park. Wheelchair access. Karaoke and discos. Lunches 12–3 (not Sun).

Stag & Hounds
Forest Road (B3034)
☎ (01344) 483553
11-11; 12-10.30 (Sun)
Courage Best, Directors; **Wadworth** 6X Ⓗ
Beautiful country pub, parts of which are 600 years old. Large inglenook fireplace in main bar with lots of nooks and crannies but beware of low beams when exploring. Historic tree in the front garden marks the spot which was once the centre of Windsor Great Park. All beers served through swan necks and sparklers.

Victoria Arms
Terrace Road North (B3018)
☎ (01344) 483856
11.30-3, 6 (6.30 Sat)-11; 12-3, 7-10.30 (Sun)
Fuller's Chiswick, London Pride, ESB, seasonal beers Ⓗ
Friendly pub in nice area serving both locals and visitors. Large bottle collection to be seen in rafters; also old Simonds of Reading advertisement. Basic selection of food plus daily specials (no food Sun eve).
Recommended.
❀ ◑ ♣ P ⅍

Bisham G1

A riverside village famous for Bisham Abbey – where the England football team train.

Bull Inn
High Street
☎ (01628) 484734/482675
11-3, 5.30-11; 12-3, 7-10.30 (Sun)
Brakspear Bitter, Special; **Wadworth** 6X Ⓗ
Restaurant (booking advised) and bar with 'olde worlde' charm. Built in 1252 as part-payment for Bisham Abbey.
Recommended.
⛼ ◑ P

Boxford B3

An attractive thatched village on the banks of the River Lambourn.

Bell Inn
(off) Rood Hill
☎ (01488) 608721
11-2.30, 6 (6.30 Fri, Sat)-11; 12-3, 7-10.30 (Sun)
Beer range varies Ⓗ
Large single-bar pub plus restaurant set at entrance to attractive Downland village. Long-standing husband/wife team are enthusiastic about their range of drinks and good food. Attractive patio area in summer.
Recommended.
⛼ Q ☋ ❀ ⛟ ◑ P

Bracknell H3

One of the country's first New Towns and now covering a vast area of East Berkshire! The town is home to many large, well-known multi-national companies and is also the HQ of the Met. Office. As far as the pub scene is concerned, Bracknell is not great for choice, although things are slowly improving.

Admiral Cunningham
Priestwood Court Road
☎ (01344) 483052
11-11; 12-10.30 (Sun)
Courage Best Ⓗ
Large hotel in middle of housing estate (behind Windlesham Road shops). Half-carpeted but pleasant saloon, games bar and restaurant, plus large garden. Named after Sir Andrew Cunningham, commander-in-chief in the Mediterranean during WW2.

Blue Lion
Broad Lane (off A322)
☎ (01344) 401051
11-11; 12-10.30 (Sun)
Draught **Bass** Ⓗ
Pub tucked away on cut-through from busy Bagshot road roundabout, mostly frequented by locals. Small patio. Sky TV. Car park at rear. Food 12–9 Mon–Fri; 12–3 Sat, Sun. Bass alternates with Fuller's London Pride.

Boot
Park Road (B3022)
☎ (01344) 454532
11-11; 12-10.30 (Sun)
Morland Original, Old Speckled Hen; **Ruddles** County Ⓗ
One of Bracknell's older and more attractive pubs with parquet floors and panelled lounge. Sports bar has large screen TV and pool table. The name has a connection with the Duke of Wellington.

Bridge House
Wokingham Road (A329)
☎ (01344) 425396
11-11; 12-10.30 (Sun)
Flowers Original; **Fuller's** London Pride; **Wadworth** 6X Ⓗ
Deceptively large pub on the outskirts of town. The lounge is very busy at lunchtimes with workers from nearby offices. The lively public bar has a large and popular games area at the rear with four pool tables.

Bull
High Street
☎ (01344) 454018
11-11; 12-10.30 (Sun)
Courage Best Ⓗ
Historic old pub, once forming part of the village High Street but now dwarfed by a number of modern structures in the town centre shopping precinct.

Cannie Man
Bywood, Hanworth
No Real Ale.

Crown Wood
Opladen Way, Crown Wood
☎ (01344) 489976
11-11; 12-10.30 (Sun)
Boddingtons Bitter Ⓗ
Estate pub next to Crown Wood shops. Real beer not always available.

Downshire Arms
Downshire Way (A329)
☎ (01344) 423585
11-11; 12-10.30 (Sun)
Boddingtons Bitter; **Fuller's** London Pride; **Marston's** Pedigree; **Wadworth** 6X Ⓗ
Beefeater family pub/restaurant situated near the Two Bridges roundabout to the west of town. Popular with the young and can be rather noisy. Large car park. Children's play area.

Fruit & Firkin
Station Road
☎ (01344) 451734
11-11; 12-10.30 (Sun)
Firkin Best, Fruit Ale, Dogbolter Ⓗ
Recently refurbished in an attempt to become more of a wine bar but still retains much of the brashness associated with the Firkin image. Food available 12–8.30 each day. Live music most Saturdays. Outside seating at front. Previously called the Market Inn. The beers come from the Flag & Firkin in Watford. *Recommended.*
❀◑◗⇌⌂

Golden Farmer

Reed's Hill (near A322), Easthampstead
☎ (01344) 420879
11-11; 12-10.30 (Sun)
Marston's Bitter, Pedigree Ⓗ
Basic estate pub with comfortable lounge and a genuine public bar with its own pool table. The 'golden' refers to fields of ripening corn.

Green Man

Crowthorne Road, Easthampstead
☎ (01344) 423667
11-11; 12-10.30 (Sun)
Courage Best, Directors; Brakspear Special Ⓗ
A genuinely old pub which has retained much character, unlike so many of the newer estate pubs in the area. Well laid out and comfortable lounge and a large public bar, popular for darts and pool. TV regularly shows sporting events. Good sized garden with children's play area.

Horse & Groom

Bagshot Road (A322)
☎ (01344) 422444
12-2.30, 5-11; 11-11 (Sat); 12-10.30 (Sun)
Draught Bass Ⓗ
Externally attractive but rather threadbare bar attached to Harvester restaurant. Food until 10 (10.30 Sat).

Newtown Pippin

Ralphs Ride, Harmans Water
No Real Ale.

Old Manor

High Street, Grenville Place (opp. Met Office)
☎ (01344) 304490
11-11; 12-10.30 (Sun)
Theakston Best; Courage Directors; guest beers; Hog's Back TEA Ⓗ
Pleasant, well appointed half-timbered building, with a number of nice alcove rooms in addition to several large bars. Priest hole. Received a new lease of life since taken over by Wetherspoon's. Previously 'Old Manor House'. No smoking in main eating area. *Recommended.*
❀ ◐◑ ♿ ⇌ ⛀ P ⊬

Prince of Wales

64 Shepherd's Lane (off B3018)
☎ (01344) 484711
11-11; 12-10.30 (Sun)
Martha Greene's Bitter; Courage Best; Greene King seasonal beer Ⓗ
Open-plan, U-shaped estate pub with large screen TV for sporting events. Occasional live entertainment. Children's play area. Food available 12–9 Mon–Fri. *Recommended.*
❀ ◐◑ P

Red Lion

High Street (near inner ring road)
☎ (01344) 454156
11-11; 12-10.30 (Sun)
Courage Best; Theakston Best; Brakspear Special Ⓗ
Deceptively large attractive old pub on the edge of town centre, surrounded by large concrete and glass structures. Popular with office workers at lunch time and a mixed, mainly young, clientele in the evenings. Very busy and noisy on Friday and Saturday evenings. Note the old milestone just outside the front door. *Recommended.*
❀ ◐◑ ⇌

Royal Foresters Hotel

London Road (A329)
☎ (01344) 884747
11-11; 12-10.30 (Sun)
Morland Original, Old Speckled Hen; Ruddles County Ⓗ
Large old roadside pub decorated in standard Beefeater style, although much of the attractive wood panelling has been retained. The restaurant is located in a separate part of the building which also improves the atmosphere of the pub. Hotel at rear. Claims to be in Ascot but it's not!

Royal Oak
Bay Road, Bullbrook (near A329)
☎ (01344) 422622
11-11; 12-10.30 (Sun)
Fuller's London Pride; Courage Best; Draught Bass Ⓗ
One of Bracknell's older buildings, sadly wrecked by refurbishment in 1998. Home cooked food. Sky TV.

Running Horse
London Road (A329)
☎ (01344) 425215
11-11; 12-10.30 (Sun)
Morland Original, Old Speckled Hen; Marston's Pedigree Ⓗ
Large roadside lounge with pool area and separate restaurant. Popular with young people.

Silver Birch
Commercial Centre, Birch Hill Road, Birch Hill
☎ (01344) 487605
12-11, 12-10.30 (Sun)
Ruddles Best, County; Morland Independent IPA, Old Speckled Hen Ⓗ
Better-than-average new estate pub comprising a comfortable lounge on two levels. Large screen TV and regular quiz nights. Children welcome Sundays only 12–7.

South Hill Park Arts Centre
Ringmead, Birch Hill
☎ (01344) 484123
11-3, 6-11; 11-11 (Sat); 12-10.30 (Sun)
Brakspear Bitter; Gales HSB; guest beers Ⓗ
Multi-arts complex housed in 18th-century mansion with its own theatre, small cinema and restaurant. Three bars in different parts of the centre. Regular special events. Children allowed until 8. Times shown are for Terrace Bar; others vary.
Recommended.
Q ❀ P

Weather Vane
Wokingham Road (B3408)
☎ (01344) 486320
11-11, 12-10.30 (Sun)
Wadworth 6X Ⓗ
New family pub/restaurant built on green field site with its adjacent Travel Inn motel in 1997. Standard formula rustic interior and Brewers Fayre menu. Children's certificate allows access until 9 pm. Disabled access and toilet. The name is a reference to the nearby meteorological office.

William Twigg
8 Great Hollands Square
No Real Ale.

Woodcutters
Bere Road, Forest Park
No Real Ale.

Bradfield D3

The village is home to Bradfield College – noted for its Greek Theatre.

Queens Head
Southend Road, Southend
☎ (0118) 974 4332
12-3, 5.30-11; 12-3, 7-10.30 (Sun)
Fuller's London Pride, ESB, seasonal beers Ⓗ
Mainly locals' pub with comfortable lounge displaying pictures from Fuller's history files and separate pool room decorated with baseball caps. Large garden with children's entertainments. Food 12–2 and 6–9 (not Mon eve). Car park.

Bray H2

Lovely Thames-side village with imposing private houses; a renowned restaurant; the old Hammer film studios and the famous 'Vicar of Bray'.

Brayfield Hotel
Windsor Road (A308)
☎ (01628) 620004/620939
11-11; 12-10.30 (Sun)
Greene King IPA Ⓗ
Small comfortable bar in sixteen-room country hotel.

Crown
High Street (B3028)
☎ (01628) 621936
11-3, 6-11; 12-3, 7-10.30 (Sun)
Courage Best, Directors; Theakston XB Ⓗ
Very old beamed pub in centre of village. Mind your head! Evening meals Tue–Sat. *Recommended.*
⌂Q❀◖◗P

Fish at Bray
Old Mill Lane (off B3028)
☎ (01628) 781111
11-3, 7-11 (Tue-Sat); 12-3 (Sun)
Fuller's London Pride Ⓗ
Although you can come in for just a drink, this is really a restaurant specialising in fresh fish. Closed Sun eve and all day Mon.

Hind's Head
High Street
☎ (01628) 626151
11-11; 12-3, 7-10.30 (Sun)
Brakspear Special; Courage Best, Fuller's London Pride; guest beer Ⓗ
Originally two 16th-century cottages. The addition of a third in 1928 as a restaurant led to today's building. Its proximity to Bray film studios led to visits from the likes of Errol Flynn and Walt Disney. The famous Vicar of Bray allegedly lived here. Ask for a tour of this famous watering hole or just wander around its oak-beamed splendour. Car park on other side of road. *Recommended.*
◖◗P

Stag at Bray
5 Windsor Road, Braywick (A308)
☎ (01628) 24100
11-3, 5.30-11; 12-10.30 (Sun)
Boddingtons Bitter; Brakspear Special; Fuller's London Pride Ⓗ
Pub near Bray Wick roundabout. Serves home-cooked food until 2.30 (lunch) and 10 (dinner).

Brimpton D4

Three Horseshoes
Brimpton Lane (OS 559648)
☎ (0118) 971 2183
11-3, 6-11; 12-3, 7-10.30 (Sun)
Fuller's London Pride, ESB; Wadworth 6X Ⓖ
Cosy, old fashioned village pub with traditional public and saloon bars and a friendly welcome. A well-cared-for pint virtually assured and cheaper than in town. If following signs from A4, take care, there are five bridges in a little over a mile. No food Sun. *Recommended.*
⌂Q❀◖⊟P

Burchetts Green G2

Crown
Burchetts Green Road
☎ (01628) 822844
11-3, 6.30-10.30; 12-3, 7-10 (Sun)
Ruddles Best; Charles Wells Bombardier Ⓗ
Small pub comprising bar attached to a restaurant which has a very good reputation. *Recommended.*
❀◖◗P

Burghfield E3

Together with Burghfield Common, the village is scattered over a wide area between the Kennet & Avon canal and the Hampshire border.

Bantam
Omers Rise
☎ (0118) 983 3016
11-3, 6-11; 12-3, 6-10.30 (Sun)
Draught Bass Ⓗ
1970s pub built in the middle of the estate it serves.

'A quart of ale is a dish fit for a king'

William Shakespeare (1564–1616)

Cunning Man
Burghfield Road, Burghfield Bridge
☎ (0118) 959 0771
12-3, 5-11; 12-3, 5-10.30 (Sun)
Draught Bass; Fuller's London Pride Ⓗ
Harvester family pub/restaurant by the Kennet & Avon canal with enormous garden. Predominantly younger clientele. Bar billiards. Disabled toilet and nappy changing facilities. Opening may be extended in summer. The name is a reference to 'trout tickling'; an ancient method of catching fish by hand.

Hatch Gate
Reading Road
☎ (0118) 983 2059
11-3, 5-11; 11-11 (Sat); 12-3, 7-10 (Sun)
Draught Bass; Morland Original; Ruddles Best; guest beer Ⓗ
Tasteful, upmarket olde worlde oak-beamed lounge dominated by food. Large inglenook. Comfortable public bar with lots of exposed brickwork. Guest beer from Butts range. *Recommended.*
P

Rising Sun
Reading Road
☎ (0118) 983 2301
11-3, 6-11; 12-11 (Sat); 12-10.30 (Sun)
Ushers Best, Founders, seasonal beers Ⓗ
A sad case of over-gutting. Young persons' activities and smoke dominate the space previously divided into several separate rooms. Children's play equipment in garden. B&B. Bar snacks only 12-2.

Six Bells
The Hatch
☎ (0118) 983 2913
11-11; 12-11 (Sun)
Courage Best; Greene King IPA; Marston's Pedigree Ⓗ
Small cosy lounge area and smoky locals' public bar in 16th-century building. Evening food on Thursday only (fish & chips). Sunday roast. Unusual sign depicts 17th-century travelling bell ringer.

Burnham H2

Almost all of Burnham is in Buckinghamshire!

Red Squirrel
150 Burnham Lane
☎ (01628) 602894
11-11; 12-10.30 (Sun)
Draught Bass Ⓗ
Harvester Steakhouse. Real ale not always available despite two handpumps. Only Burnham pub in Berkshire.

Caversham F2

Situated over the Thames from Reading, Caversham is a mixture of old terraced houses, new estates and large riverside properties. Caversham Court and St Annes Well are worth seeing and there are a good number of pubs in the area, with something to suit most drinkers. There is also a wide selection of restaurants and take-aways.

Baron Cadogan
22–24 Prospect Street (A4155)
☎ (0118) 947 0626
11-11; 12-10.30 (Sun)
Fuller's London Pride; Courage Directors; guest beers Ⓗ
Large open-plan Wetherspoon's pub which has proven a great asset to the area. Named after the family who originally occupied Caversham Park.
Recommended.
Q

Black Horse
Kidmore End Road, Emmer Green
☎ (0118) 947 4111
11-11; 12-10.30 (Sun)
Courage Best; Brakspear Bitter; Wadworth 6X Ⓗ
Basic, down-to-earth local retaining some of its original charm. 'Jug and Bottle' separates the two bars. Beers served through swan necks and sparklers.

Clifton Arms
12 Gosbrook Road (B3349)
☎ (0118) 947 1775
11-11; 12-10.30 (Sun)
Brakspear Bitter, Special Ⓗ
Unassuming Brakspear tied house with L-shaped bar and separate restaurant at rear. *Recommended.*
❀ ◖ ♣ ⚟

Fox & Hounds
51 Gosbrook Road (B3349)
No Real Ale.

Gardener's Arms
48 Surley Row, Emmer Green
☎ (0118) 947 2757
11.30-3.30, 5.30-11; 11.30-11 (Fri, Sat); 12-10.30 (Sun)
Morland Original, Old Speckled Hen, Draught **Bass, Ruddles** County Ⓗ
Smart pub hidden away in upmarket residential area. Meals lunchtimes and evenings; no-smoking dining area. Pool, regular live music and skittle alley. *Recommended.*
❀ ◖◗ P ⚟

Golden Key
129 Queen's Road (off B3349)
☎ (0118) 947 3409
11-11; 12-10.30 (Sun)
Brakspear Bitter, Special Ⓗ
Backstreet locals' pub with open-plan lounge and public bar areas. Recently refurbished under new management.

Griffin
10/12 Church Road (A4074)
☎ (0118) 947 5018
11-11; 12-10.30 (Sun)
Theakston XB; **Courage** Best, Directors; guest beers Ⓗ
Olde-worlde-style conversion to Chef & Brewer brand. Food-oriented but one guest beer usually from independent brewers. Candle-lit tables for diners. All beers served through swan necks and sparklers. *Recommended.*
❀ ◖◗ P

Grosvenor
109 Kidmore Road, Caversham Heights (off A4074)
☎ (0118) 947 4073
12-11; 12-10.30 (Sun)
Draught **Bass; Worthington** Best; **Fuller's** London Pride Ⓗ
Very large, smart and comfortable food-orientated pub with several different eating and drinking areas. Indoor play area for children (no smoking). Families welcome. *Recommended.*
👶 ❀ ◖◗ P ⚟

Miller's Arms
1 Paddock Road
☎ (0118) 947 2445
11-3, 5.30-11; 11-11 (Sat); 12-3, 7-10.30 (Sun)
Morland Original; **Ruddles** Best, County Ⓗ
Comfortable wood-panelled locals' pub with large garden, function room and skittle alley. Reasonably priced lunchtime meals and toasted sandwiches.

Piper's Island Riverside Bar & Restaurant
Piper's Island, Bridge Street (A4155)
☎ (0118) 948 4573
12-3, 5-11; 12-11 (Fri, Sat); 12-10.30 (Sun)
Flowers Original; **Wadworth** 6X; **Brakspear** Bitter Ⓗ
Lively bar on an island in the River Thames reached by footbridge from Caversham bridge. Outside terrace with fine riverside views. Upstairs 'Steamer's Bistro' doubles as a function room for wedding receptions, etc. Departure point for riverboat cruises. *Recommended.*
❀ ◖◗

Prince of Wales
76 Prospect Street
☎ (0118) 947 2267
11-3, 6-11; 11-11 (Sat); 12-10.30 (Sun)
Brakspear Bitter, Special, Old, seasonal beers Ⓗ
A lively, boisterous and friendly local near the centre. Children welcome for Sunday lunch. Occasional live music. *Recommended.*
❀ ◖ ♣ P

Red Cow
Star Road
No Real Ale.

Star
South View Avenue (A4155)
No Real Ale.

Traveller's Rest
Henley Road (A4155)
☎ (0118) 947 9441
11-11; 12-10.30 (Sun)
Brakspear Bitter, Special; **Boddingtons** Bitter Ⓗ
Large Brewers Fayre pub with several distinct drinking/eating areas, some wood-panelled. Food available all day. Function room. *Recommended.*
◖◗ P ⍉

White Horse
Kidmore End Road, Emmer Green
☎ (0118) 947 3741
11-11; 12-10.30 (Sun)
Greene King IPA, Triumph, Abbot; Draught **Bass** Ⓗ
Revitalised following change of ownership to Greene King. Extended into adjoining cottage and smartly refurbished throughout. Pool table tucked away from main bar. *Recommended.*
❀ ◖◗ ♣ P

Chaddleworth B2

Ibex
Tower Hill/Sheephouse Way
☎ (01488) 638311
11.30-3, 6-11; 12-4, 7-10.30 (Sun)
Charles Wells Bombardier; **Ruddles** Best Bitter Ⓗ
Traditional country pub with three separate bars plus restaurant, located in quiet downland village in heart of horse breeding area. Pleasant garden and patio. Well-kept real ale and good food. Named after a species of wild goat that lives in the Alps. *Recommended.*
♨ Q ♞ ❀ ◖◗ ⊟ P

Chalvey J2

A western suburb of Slough.

Courtyard Hotel
Church Street
No Real Ale.

Flags
43 Church Street
No Real Ale.

Foresters Arms
26 Chalvey Road West
☎ (01753) 523087
11-11; 12-10.30 (Sun)
John Smith's Bitter Ⓗ
Two-bar community local.

Garibaldi
6 The Green
No Real Ale.

Keys
35 High Street
☎ (01753) 520519
11-11; 12-10.30 (Sun)
Young's Bitter Ⓗ
Locals' pub with two bars; real ale in lounge only.

Prince of Wales
Windsor Road
No Real Ale.

Chapel Row D3

Bladebone
(OS 570696)
☎ (0118) 971 2326
11-2.30, 6-11; 12-3, 7-10.30 (Sun)
Flowers IPA; **Brakspear** Bitter Ⓗ
Down-to-earth public bar and comfortable lounge where food dominates in this village centre pub. A conservatory at the back is also mainly used by diners. Reasonably priced menu. Large secluded garden has swings and other children-friendly activities. The name comes from the bone of a prehistoric animal found nearby.

Charvil F2

Land's End
Park Lane (OS 781748)
☎ (0118) 934 0700
11-3, 5-11; 12-10.30 (Sun)
Brakspear Bitter, Special, seasonal beers Ⓗ
Cosy bar and separate restaurant in remote, semi-rural setting. Major alterations summer 1999.

Open all day summer weekends. *Recommended.*
❀ ◐ ⊞ P

Wee Waif
Old Bath Road (A3032/A4)
☎ (0118) 944 0066
11-11; 12-10.30 (Sun)
Morland Original, Tanner's Jack; Ruddles County Ⓗ
Artist's Fare bar and restaurant, part of motel and conference centre complex. The unusual name derives from a local philanthropist, Edward Polehampton. Bar billiards. Food every day until 10.

Chieveley C2

Probably most known for its traffic reports (at the junction of the A34 and M4) the village has sadly just lost another of its pubs with Morland closing the Wheatsheaf.

Blue Boar
North Heath (B4494)
(OS 455741)
☎ (01635) 248236
11-3, 6-11; 12-3, 7-10.30 (Sun)
Fuller's London Pride, Wadworth 6X Ⓗ
Historic pub mentioned in Civil War accounts of Battles of Newbury. Splendid view over Winterbourne Valley so that the M4 is almost unnoticed. This isolated spot is, nevertheless, only 4 miles north of Newbury and 2 miles from the A34/M4 junction, hence major recent extensions providing large accommodation and restaurant business. *Recommended.*
⌂ Q ❀ ⊨ ◐ P

Olde Red Lion (Ye)
Green Lane
☎ (01635) 248379
11-3, 6-11; 12-3, 7-10.30 (Sun)
Arkell's 3B, Kingsdown Ⓗ
Long bar leads to quieter seating area and then large restaurant separate from main bar. A small area is given over to pool and darts. *Recommended.*
⌂ ❀ ◐ ♿ ♣ P

Cippenham J2

A western suburb of Slough.

Barleycorn
151 Lower Cippenham Lane
☎ (01628) 603115
12-2.30, 5.30-11; 12-11 (Sat); 12-10.30 (Sun)
Courage Best, Directors; guest beer Ⓗ
Small cosy one-bar pub with a touch of the shamrock about it. Guest beer from Rebellion and Whitbread range.

Copthorne Hotel
Tuns Lane roundabout, Cippenham Lane
☎ (01753) 516222
11-11; 12-10.30 (Sun)
Courage Best, Marston's Pedigree Ⓗ
Characterless hotel bar: clean, modern and without atmosphere. Beer prices expensive. Real ale in 'Duke's Bar'.

Earl of Cornwall
Weekes Drive, Cippenham Lane
☎ (01753) 578333
11-11; 12-10.30 (Sun)
Marston's Pedigree; Boddingtons Bitter Ⓗ
Large modern two-bar pub which has recently undergone a substantial refurbishment.

Huntercombe
595 Bath Road
☎ (01628) 663177
12-11; 12-10.30 (Sun)
Courage Best, Directors; Marston's Pedigree Ⓗ
Two-bar locals' pub with strong Irish flavour. Popular music nights in separate music room.

Kings Head
149 Lower Cippenham Lane
☎ (01628) 605180
11-11; 12-10.30 (Sun)
Flowers Original; Boddingtons Bitter Ⓗ
Old, beamed and dimly-lit but welcoming local. Family room and garden. Lunchtimes and evening (book) meals.

Long Barn
Cippenham Lane
☎ (01753) 521396
11.30-11; 12-11 (Sat); 12-10.30 (Sun)
Courage Best, Directors; **Theakston** Best Ⓗ
Converted 17th-century barn with separate restaurant. Patio seating area.

Swan
140 Lower Cippenham Lane
No Real Ale.

White Horse
359 Bath Road (A4)
☎ (01628) 603666
11-11; 12-10.30 (Sun)
Marston's Pedigree; **Tetley** Bitter; guest beer Ⓗ
Spacious Big Steak restaurant/pub, half a mile from Burnham station. The Wacky Warehouse provides a welcome change for the kids from being dragged around the nearby retail park. Large car park and garden at rear. Guest beer changes weekly.

Clay Hill D3

Travellers Rest
Cock Lane
No Real Ale. May change following alterations to cellar.

Cold Ash C3

Expanding village to the north of Thatcham whose two pubs are next door to each other.

Castle
Cold Ash Hill
☎ (01635) 863232
12-3, 6-11; 12-3, 6-10.30 (Sun)
Tetley Bitter; **Courage** Best; guest beers Ⓗ
Friendly local with large bar and area set aside for dining during the evening. Regular beers served through swan necks and sparklers although up to three guests which are not. TV for major sports events. Lunches every day. Evening meals Tue–Sat. *Recommended.*
❀ ◑ ♣ P

Spotted Dog
Gladstone Lane
☎ (01635) 862458
12-3, 6.30-11; 12-3, 6.30-10.30 (Sun)
Fuller's London Pride; guest beers Ⓗ
Smart but comfortable village pub offering an extensive food menu with separate dining room, although most customers seem to prefer eating in the bar. Genuine free house with up to three guest beers, usually from independent breweries. Local darts following. Patio area at front. Food from 12–2 and 7–9.30. *Recommended.*
❀ ◑ ♣ P

Colnbrook J2

A thriving village when on the old coaching routes but its importance diminished with the advent of the railways. The Colne brook once was the boundary between Buckinghamshire and Middlesex; more recently the confused village was partly in Surrey but is now on the eastern extremities of Berkshire. The Ostrich is one of the oldest pubs in the country.

Crown
Old Bath Road
☎ (01753) 682026
12-11; 12-10.30 (Sun)
Fuller's London Pride Ⓗ
Large single-bar pub with conservatory suitable for families.

Golden Cross
Poyle Road, Poyle
☎ (01753) 682231
12-11; 12-10.30 (Sun)
Greene King IPA, seasonal beers; guest beer Ⓗ
Old one-bar pub in shadow of reservoir. Caters predominantly for workers from the industrial estate opposite. Guest beers not always available.

Greyhound
Colnbrook By-Pass (A4)
Closed – due to reopen as a nightclub.

Olde George
146 High Street
☎ (01753) 682010
11-3, 5-11; 12-3, 7-11 (Sat); 12-3, 7-10.30 (Sun)
Courage Best; Ushers Best, Founders, seasonal beers Ⓗ
Genuinely historic old coaching inn, well run by long-standing landlord. Now only one bar but divided by several screens and panels. Board games available. Opens at 7.30 for breakfast (Mon–Fri). Occasional extended opening Sat eve. *Recommended.*
🏰❀⇄◖◗P

Ostrich
High Street
☎ (01753) 682628
11-3, 5.30-11; 12-10.30 (Sun)
Courage Best, Directors; Marston's Pedigree Ⓗ
Parts of this ancient coaching inn date back to 1106, making it reputedly England's third oldest pub. Its grisly past includes a landlord who murdered his guests. A number of comfortable seating areas are served from a small bar. Extensive food menu (including Ostrich steaks!) *Recommended.*
🏰◖◗P

Punchbowl
Bath Road
☎ (01753) 682683
12-3, 5-11; 11-11 (Fri); 12-11 (Sat); 12-3, 7-10.30 (Sun)
Draught Bass; Fuller's London Pride Ⓗ
Small, one-bar pub at eastern end of village: first and last pub in Berkshire.

Quality Hotel
Bath Road
No Real Ale.

Red Lion
High Street
☎ (01753) 682685
12-3, 7-11; 12-3, 7-10.30 (Sun)
Ushers Best, Founders Ⓗ
Small traditional three-bar pub which dates back over 500 years. Wood panelling and original bench seating.

Star & Garter
Park Street
☎ (01753) 682157
11-11; 12-10.30 (Sun)
Courage Best, Morland Old Speckled Hen Ⓗ
Small, friendly, listed pub with original beams. River Colne runs at the bottom of the garden. Until 1995 this was the only Colnbrook pub in Surrey.

Compton C2

The remains of the defunct Didcot, Newbury & Southampton railway line can still be seen through the village.

Swan Hotel
Cheap Street
☎ (01635) 578269
11-11; 12-10.30 (Sun)
Ruddles Best, County; Draught Bass Ⓗ
Large hotel with cosy lounge and public bars, games and function rooms. Six bedrooms shortly to become twelve. Food all day every day: the owner is a chef.

Cookham H1

A delightful Thames-side town with strong connections with the artist Stanley Spencer. There are excellent views from nearby Winter Hill (see Cookham Dean). The pubs are scattered over a wide area between the station, the common and the river.

Bel & the Dragon
High Street
☎ (01628) 521263
11-3, 6-11; 11-3, 6-10.30 (Sun)
Brakspear Bitter, Courage Best, Marston's Pedigree Ⓗ
Beautiful cosy old pub which dates back to 1470. Separate restaurant. The name derives from a biblical reference.

JOIN CAMRA TODAY!
see page 126

Bounty
Riverside (on towpath)
☎ (01628) 520056
12-10.30
Brakspear Bitter; **Rebellion** Mutiny Ⓗ
Situated on the Cookham side of the river, this pub is indeed a gem of the Thames. The beer is delivered by river. The bar is the prow of a boat and a nautical theme dominates. The ferry, previously the only access, is now used only for deliveries since footbridge opened. (Cross railway bridge on foot from Bourne End station; pub is 50 yards along towpath.)
Recommended.

Cookham Tavern
Lower Road
☎ (01628) 529519
11-2.30, 5.30-11 (Mon-Thur); 11.30-11 (Fri, Sat); 12-10.30 (Sun)
Brakspear Bitter, **Greene King** Abbot, **Castle Eden** Bitter Ⓗ
Welcoming and comfortable local close to the station. Food available until 7 on Sun.
Recommended.

Crown
The Moor (B4447)
☎ (01628) 520163
11-11; 12-10.30 (Sun)
Courage Best, **Charles Wells** Bombardier; guest beer Ⓗ
Interesting old pub to the west of Cookham High Street, popular with walkers. Home-cooked food includes excellent steak and kidney pies.
Recommended.

Ferry
Sutton Road (A4094)
☎ (01628) 525123
12-2.30, 5-11; 12-10.30 (Sun)
Draught **Bass** Ⓗ
Harvester pub/restaurant close to Cookham bridge. Folk club Wed eves.

King's Arms
High Street
☎ (01628) 530667
11-11; 12-10.30 (Sun)
Boddingtons Bitter, **Marston's** Pedigree Ⓗ
Beefeater inn with large garden. Food available lunch and eves and all day Sat/Sun.

Old Anchor
The Pound
Closed at the time of survey.

Old Swan Uppers
The Pound (B4447)
☎ (01628) 521324
11-11; 12-10.30 (Sun)
Greene King IPA, Abbot Ⓗ
One-hundred-and-fifty-year-old free house with beams and alcoves. Restaurant area and conservatory where children are welcome. Warm and cosy.
Recommended.

P

Spencers
The Pound (B4447)
☎ (01628) 522793
11-11; 11-3, 6-11 (Sat); 12-3, 6-10.30 (Sun)
Morland Original; **Ruddles** County; guest beer Ⓗ
Bar and restaurant with purple walls and a rather spartan modern decor.

Cookham Dean H1

Pretty area of hills and woodlands often known as 'Little Switzerland'; with excellent views across to Marlow and Maidenhead.

Chequers Brasserie
Dean Lane
☎ (01628) 481232
12-3, 5.30-11; 12-4, 7-10.30 (Sun)
Morland Original; **Ruddles** County Ⓗ
More of a bistro than a pub.

Inn on the Green
Old Cricket Common
☎ (01628) 482638
12-3, 5.30-11; 12-3, 7-10.30 (Sun)
Brakspear Bitter; **Fuller's** London Pride; guest beer Ⓗ
Cosy bar with restaurant within

Horns, Crazies Hill

an inn with eight bedrooms. Refurbishment in 1999 improved disabled access. *Recommended.*
🏰 Q ❀ 🛏 ◑ ♿ P

Jolly Farmer
Church Road
☎ (01628) 482905
11.30-3, 5.30-11; 12-5, 7-10.30 (Sun)
Courage Best; guest beers Ⓗ
Beautiful little country pub, now a friendly free house. Bought 'by the village, for the village'. Two guest beers usually available.

Uncle Tom's Cabin
Hills Lane
☎ (01628) 483339
11-3, 5.30-11; 12-3, 7-10.30 (Sun)
Benskin's Bitter; **Marston's** Pedigree, guest beer Ⓗ
Three-hundred-and-fifty-year-old pub on top of hill. Many interesting gold discs included in decor. Named after a novel published in 1852. *Recommended.*
🏰 ❀ ◑ P

Cox Green H2

Barley Mow
Cox Green Lane
☎ (01628) 629986
11.30-2.30, 5.30-11; 11.30-11 (Fri); 11-11.30 (Sat); 12-3, 7.30-10.30 (Sun)
Fuller's London Pride, ESB; guest beers Ⓗ
Cosy village pub with friendly landlord who is interested in real ale. Two guest beers usually available. *Recommended.*
❀ ◑ ♿ ♣ P

Foresters
Cox Green Lane
☎ (01628) 770564
11.30-11; 12-10.30 (Sun)
Brakspear Bitter; **Courage** Best Ⓗ
Cosy pub in winter; pleasant garden in summer.

Thatched Cottage
Cannon Lane
☎ (01628) 822347
11-11; 12-10.30 (Sun)
Brakspear Special; **Courage** Best; **Greene King** IPA Ⓗ
Nearest pub to Woodlands Park, close to bridges over and under the railway. Popular for food at lunchtimes.

Crazies Hill G2

Horns
(OS 799809) (near A321)
☎ (0118) 940 1416
11.30-2.30, 5.30-11; 12-3, 6-10.30 (Sun)
Brakspear Bitter, Special, Old Ale Ⓗ
Attractive country pub set in its own grounds. The bar has a homely feel with real fires during the winter months; decorated by rugby and other sporting memorabilia. A large barn at the end of the pub is used as a restaurant. Large garden with children's play area. No food Sunday evening. *Recommended.*
🏰 Q ◑ P

Crowthorne G4

The village has links with The Duke of Wellington, which is reflected in many of the pub names. Wellington College (a public school) can be seen on the long walk from the railway station.

Crowthorne Inn

High Street (A3095)
☎ NOT LISTED
11–11; 12–10.30 (Sun)
Beer range varies Ⓗ
Locals' pub with interesting decor. Pool table and TV in public bar and regular quiz nights in saloon. Now a free house but still shows signs of its Friary Meux past.

Iron Duke

254 High Street
☎ (01344) 772568
11–11; 12–10.30 (Sun)
Courage Best; Fuller's London Pride Ⓗ
Large and lively games room with a smaller lounge. Children's play equipment in garden. Basic food menu available all day. Food available 12–2.30. Happy hours 4–7 Mon–Thur. Named after the nickname of the Duke of Wellington.

Last Shoe

63 Church Street
☎ (01344) 777771
12–3, 7–11 (closed Sat lunch/all day Sun)
Fuller's London Pride; guest beer Ⓗ
Smart restaurant with a gambling theme and a small bar intended mainly for pre-dinner drinks but casual drinkers are made welcome. Weekend opening may be extended.

Olde Prince (Ye)

High Street
☎ (01344) 772241
11–11; 12–10.30 (Sun)
Brakspear Special; Courage Best Ⓗ
Young persons' venue with 'knights in armour' theme. Several rooms knocked into one. Previously called Prince Alfred.

Waterloo Hotel

Dukes Ride (B3348)
☎ (01344) 777711
11–3, 6–11; 11–11 (Fri, Sat); 12–3, 6–10.30 (Sun)
Flowers Original; Wadworth 6X Ⓗ
Arthur's Bar and Copenhagen's brasserie: refurbished in 1997 in arty bare boards style. Large painting of Wellington and Blucher after Waterloo. Beer expensive. TV sport.

Who'd a Tho't it!

Nine Mile Ride, Easthampstead (B3430)
☎ (01344) 772125
11.30–3, 6–11; 12–3.30, 6–10.30 (Sun)
Morland Original; Ruddles Best; Greene King Abbot Ⓗ
Wooden floors in a comfortable lounge with separate restaurant area. Basic public bar with bar billiards table. Front garden with children's play area. Unusual name has several possible meanings but definitely not the one depicted on the pub sign.

Curridge C3

Bunk

(off B4009, marked 'Curridge village only', OS 492723)
☎ (01635) 200400
11–11; 12–10.30 (Sun)
Arkell's 3B; Fuller's London Pride; Wadworth 6X; guest beer Ⓗ
Very food-oriented, pricey establishment. Pleasant old building with well-to-do clientele and good quality food and drink. Attractive patio. Food 11–2.30, 6.30–10. *Recommended.*
❀ ◐ P

Datchet J2

Noted as being the traditional site of the ducking of Shakespeare's Falstaff in the River Thames.

Manor Hotel

1 High Street
☎ (01753) 543442
11-3, 5-11; 12-3, 7-10.30 (Sun)
Courage Best, Directors Ⓗ
Small hotel situated on village green. Restaurant and bar food menu available.

Morning Star

The Green
☎ (01753) 591399
11-11; 12-10.30 (Sun)
Ushers Best, Founders, seasonal beers Ⓗ
Recently refurbished one-bar pub with wood panelling. Small dining area upstairs. Food available 12–9.30 (6 Sun). Named after famous GWR locomotive. *Recommended.*
❀ ◐ ◗ ⥄

Rising Sun

147 Horton Road (B376)
☎ (01753) 541309
2-11; 12-11 (Fri, Sat); 12-3, 7-10.30 (Sun)
Charles Wells Eagle Ⓗ
Local pub with small customer base. Recently changed hands so details may change.

Royal Stag

The Green
☎ (01753) 548218
11-11; 12-10.30 (Sun)
Ind Coope Burton Ale; Marston's Pedigree; Tetley Bitter; guest beer Ⓗ
Old pub of uncertain age but has been an alehouse since mid-1600s. Among the curiosities is a mysterious print of a child's hand which sometimes appears on the window facing the churchyard. In 1966 a tombstone was unearthed in the cellar to William Herbert who died in 1705. Comfortable and justifiably popular. Check the panelling made from champagne cases. Quiz nights. Patio area. No food Sun eve. *Recommended.*
♔ ❀ ◐ ◗ ⊟ ⥄ ♣ P

Donnington C3

The village is strongly connected with the Civil War and the Battle of Newbury in the 17th century. Also of note is the fact that the local CAMRA branch forced Whitbread to revert to the original name of the village pub after the brewery had changed it to one of their silly themes!

Castle

Oxford Road (B4494)
☎ (01635) 40615
12-11.30; 12-10.30 (Sun)
Flowers Original; Wadworth 6X Ⓗ
Spacious interior largely devoted to selling food of standard chain restaurant quality. Named after nearby Donnington Castle, demolished by Cromwell in the Battle of Newbury. Adequate parking makes sensible starting point for exploring castle ruins and nearby Donnington Park nature reserve. A little over one mile from Newbury market square and railway station.

Fox & Hounds

Oxford Road (OS 471706)
☎ (01635) 40540
11-11; 12-10.30 (Sun)
Arkell's 3B, Kingsdown, seasonal beers Ⓗ
Quiet, comfortable pub with single bar plus restaurant and nearby golf course. Recently acquired and renovated by the Swindon brewer having previously been a free house. Has settled down after disturbance following recent bypass construction. Food 12–3, 7–9. *Recommended.*
♔ Q ◐ ◗ ♣ P

'What is drinking? A mere pause from thinking'

Lord Byron (1788–1824)

Three Horseshoes

Castle Lane (off B4494)
☎ (01635) 41366
11-2.30, 6-11; 12-10.30 (Sun)
Courage Directors; **Ushers** Best Ⓗ
Quiet, comfortable one-bar village pub. Patio area beside stream with children's play area. Recommended for families. Lunchtime meals served every day. *Recommended.*
Q ❀ ◖ ♿ ♣ P

Earley F3

A southern suburb of Reading (see also Lower Earley).

George

479 Wokingham Road
☎ (0118) 926 1844
11-11; 12-10.30 (Sun)
Courage Best, Directors; **Theakston** XB; **Wadworth** 6X; guest beer Ⓗ
Old building, much extended and largely open plan. Separate restaurant with late supper licence. Very large riverside terrace and garden. Guest beer is very expensive.

Maiden Over

Silverdale Road (near A329)
☎ (0118) 926 5392
11.30-3, 5.30-11 (Mon-Thur); 11.30-11 (Fri, Sat); 12-10.30 (Sun)
Courage Best; **Wadworth** 6X; **Brakspear** Special; **Marston's** Pedigree Ⓗ
An estate pub which has friendlier atmosphere than most. Two pool tables dominate the public bar. The Ken Barrington lounge includes a dining section. Food is served 12–2.30 and 6–11 (not Sun eve).

Roebuck

Auckland Road
☎ (0118) 926 2226
12-11; 12-10.30 (Sun)
Morland Independent IPA, Original Ⓗ
Wood-panelled lounge is adorned with plates and animal pictures. Separate games room has pool table and large screen TV. Happy hour 7–9 Wed, Sat. Food available lunchtimes and each evening except Sun.

East Garston A2

Queens Arms Hotel

Newbury Road
No Real Ale.

East Ilsley C2

The village lies in a fold in the Downs (just off the busy A34) and is connected with racehorse training, although it was once the principal wool and sheep market in West Berkshire.

Crown & Horns

Compton Road
☎ (01635) 281205 (pub)/ (01635) 281545 (hotel)
11-11; 12-10.30 (Sun)
Morland Original; **Ruddles** County; guest beers Ⓗ
Amazing old hotel, with various bars almost totally unspoilt apart from the unnecessary addition of music and TVs. Ten-room hotel, all en suite. Food available 12–2, 6–10. Small separate no-smoking restaurant. Skittle alley. Patio area. Usually four guest beers available, mainly from independent breweries. *Recommended.*
♉ ❀ ⛟ ◖◗ ♣ P ⚡

'Who comes here? A Grenadier. What does he want? A pot of beer'

Charles Dickens (1812–1859) 'Our Mutual Friend'

Star
High Street
☎ (01635) 281215
11-2.30, 6-11; 12-2.30, 7-10.30 (Sun)
Ushers Best; **Arkell's** 3B; guest beer Ⓗ
Friendly and comfortable locals' pub, up the hill from village centre, hence its nickname 'up the top'. Three large fireplaces included in its several rooms. Shove ha'penny board.

Swan
High Street
☎ (01635) 281238
11-3, 6-11; 12-3, 6-10.30 (Sun)
Morland Original; **Ruddles** County; **Charles Wells** Bombardier Ⓗ
Acquired by Morland in 1843 when their brewery was in neighbouring West Ilsley, now a hotel offering a range of accommodation. Separate restaurant or food served in bar at most times. Award-winning garden. Beer rather pricey.

Eastbury A2

A pretty little village nestling in the Lambourn Valley. The pigeon cote at Pigeonhouse Farm is said to have 999 nesting holes under its pyramidal roof.

Plough Inn
(OS 343775)
☎ (01488) 71312
11-3, 7-11; 12-3, 7-10.30 (Sun)
Morland Original, Old Speckled Hen; Draught **Bass**; **Flowers** Original; **Butts** Barbus Barbus; guest beers Ⓗ
A popular village pub in West Berkshire serving a wide selection of guest ales. Bar and restaurant meals available.

'Dost thou think, because thou art virtuous, there shall be no more cakes and ale?'

William Shakespeare (1564–1616)

Enborne B3

Another village associated with the Battle of Newbury during the English Civil War. It was in this area that Lord Falkland was killed.

Craven Arms
Red Hill (OS 427647)
☎ (01635) 253336
11-11; 12-10.30 (Sun)
Wadworth Henry's IPA, 6X; **Badger** Tanglefoot, seasonal beers; guest beers Ⓗ
Large family-oriented country pub serving good food. Children's play facilities in garden plus caged pets. Regular charity fund raising. No food Sun eve. *Recommended.*

Eton J2

A short walk across the pedestrian bridge from Windsor lies Eton and its world-famous public school (founded in 1440), which dominates this pleasant riverside town, and where the schoolboys, in their unique uniforms, can be seen parading around the streets between classes. A visit to the magnificent Gothic Chapel is a must and the 18th-century High Street is well worth exploring as it has some fine architecture including The Cockpit – where King Charles II patronised cock-fighting. Most of the pubs are near to the bridge in the High Street.

Christopher Hotel
110 High Street
☎ (01753) 852359
11-11; 12-10.30 (Sun)
Adnams Bitter; **Brakspear** Bitter; guest beer Ⓗ
Old pub which is now the bar for the adjoining hotel. Quiet and relaxed atmosphere most of the time. Guest beer usually from Adnams seasonal beer range. Named after the patron saint of travellers.

Crown & Cushion
84 High Street
☎ (01753) 861531
11-11; 12-10.30 (Sun)
Courage Best; Marston's Pedigree; Morland Old Speckled Hen; John Smith's Bitter Ⓗ
Little old two-bar pub mostly populated by locals.

Henry VI
High Street
☎ (01753) 670134
11-11; 12-10.30 (Sun)
Brakspear Bitter; Fuller's London Pride; Flowers Original Ⓗ
Long, split-level pub now named after the founder of Eton College and decorated with pictures of the school, its incumbents and its history. Near Windsor & Eton Riverside station.

Hogshead
77 High Street
☎ (01753) 861797
11-11; 12-10.30 (Sun)
Brakspear Abroad Cooper; Marston's Pedigree; Fuller's London Pride; Boddingtons Bitter; Wadworth 6X; Timothy Taylor Landlord Ⓗ; **guest beers** Ⓗ/Ⓖ
Hogshead alehouse with various intimate seating areas. Its location is just over the Thames from Windsor and attracts a strong tourist flavour to complement its local popularity. *Recommended.*
⛫ ❀ ◐ ◑ ≠ ⏻

New College
55 High Street
☎ (01753) 865516
11-11; 12-10.30 (Sun)
Badger IPA, Best, Robert's Pride, Tanglefoot Ⓗ
The former College Arms was taken over and renovated by Hall & Woodhouse in summer 1998, thereby reintroducing real ale into Eton's only lager emporium. The large open-plan bar has been changed to a comfortable multi-section bar by the judicious use of wood partitions. Children welcome until early evening. Food available until 9.30. Near Windsor & Eton Riverside station. Outside patio area. *Recommended.*
❀ ◐ ◑ ≠

Waterman's Arms
Brocas Street
☎ (01753) 861001
11-2.30, 6-11; 11-3, 6-11 (Sat); 12-10.30 (Sun)
Brakspear Bitter; Courage Best, Directors; Greene King IPA; John Smith's Bitter; guest beers Ⓗ
Sixteenth-century pub near the Thames which offers a friendly welcome. The no-smoking room has a boating theme which traces the history of Eton rowing club. Extensive menu of traditional pub grub is available, served in either the bar or restaurant area. No food Sun eve. Parking difficult. Near Windsor & Eton Riverside station. *Recommended.*
⛫ Q ◐ ◑ ≠ ♣ ⍉

Eton Wick J2

A residential village between Eton and Slough with a good choice of beers for the area.

Greyhound
The Walk
☎ (01753) 863925
12-3, 5.30-11; 12-11 (Sat); 12-3, 7-10.30 (Sun)
Morland Original; Ruddles Best; Draught Bass Ⓗ
Traditional village pub with friendly atmosphere. Popular with locals, walkers and cyclists. Good home-cooked food. Pets welcome. Food served 12–2.15, 5.30–9.30 and all day Sat. *Recommended.*
❀ ◐ ◑ ♣ P

'Don't you know drinking is a slow death? So who's in a hurry?'

Robert Benchley

Pickwick
32 Eton Wick Road (B3026)
☎ (01753) 861713
12-3, 6-11; 12-4, 7-10.30 (Sun)
Young's Bitter, Special, seasonal beers Ⓗ
Traditional locals' pub, acquired by Young's some years ago. Relatively close to the Thames and popular with walkers. Quiz nights Tue and Sun. Food is traditional with an Italian influence. Occasional live music. No food Tue and Sun eve. *Recommended.*
Q❀◖◗P

Shepherd's Hut
Eton Wick Road (B3026)
☎ (01753) 853297
11-11; 12-10.30 (Sun)
Fuller's London Pride, ESB, seasonal beers Ⓗ
Large, one-bar Fuller's tied house in the centre of the village. Popular with locals. Pleasant patio area at front and large car park at rear. Bar snacks served all day. *Recommended.*
⛫❀◖◗♿♣P

Three Horseshoes
44 Eton Wick Road
☎ (01753) 867889
11-11; 12-10.30 (Sun)
Courage Best Ⓗ
Oldest pub in the village.

Eversley F4

The village straddles the Berkshire/Hampshire border (which is a stream near the Tally Ho pub). Charles Kingsley – author of *The Water Babies* – is buried in the churchyard.

Tally Ho
Fleet Hill (A327)
☎ (0118) 973 2134
11-3, 6-11; 11-11 (Fri, Sat); 12-10.30 (Sun)
Draught Bass; Courage Best; Wadworth 6X Ⓗ
Comfortable lounge bar and annexe. Young and old clientele. Extensive, reasonably priced menu. Food lunchtimes and evenings (not Sun, Mon eve). Regular winner of quiz leagues. Children's play galleon outside.

Fifield H2

Fifield Inn
Fifield Road
☎ (01628) 626512
11-2.30 (3 Sat), 6-11 (not Mon); 12-3, 6.30-10.30 (Sun)
Morland Original; Ruddles County; guest beer Ⓗ
Modernised country pub. Entrance through a patio covered in grape vines and clematis. Separate dining area. Sunday night jazz (dixie and swing). Restricted menu Sun eve (available until 9.30).

Hare & Hounds
Fifield Road
☎ (01628) 622763
11-11; 12-10.30 (Sun)
Guest beers Ⓗ
Extended 19th-century village local retaining a good pub atmosphere, much frequented by people from nearby farms and offices. Children welcome in conservatory area until 8. Despite their appearance, the 'barrel ends' do dispense real ale. Food served 12–2.30 and 7–9.30 (Mon/Sat) and 12–3 (Sun). Usually two to four beers available. *Recommended.*
❀◖◗P

Finchampstead G4

There are some glorious views over three counties from the top of Finchampstead ridges.

Greyhound
Longwater Road
☎ (0118) 973 2305
11-11; 12-10.30 (Sun)
Fuller's London Pride; Wadworth 6X Ⓗ
Brewers Fayre pub/restaurant with chintzy decor. Children's certificate.

JOIN CAMRA TODAY!
see page 126

White Hart, Hampstead Norreys

Queen's Oak
Church Lane (off B3016)
☎ (0118) 973 4855
11-2.30, 6-11; 11.30-3 (4 summer), 6.30-11 (Sat); 12-3, 7-10.30 (Sun)
Brakspear Bitter, Special, Old, seasonal beer Ⓗ
Excellent country pub tucked away in hamlet opposite church. Nice garden for children and large key fob collection in bar. Snacks plus specials with pizza a speciality. No food Sunday evening. *Recommended.*
❀ ◐ ◑ ⊞ ⛺ ♣ P ⚟

Frilsham D3

Pot Kiln
(OS 553732)
☎ (01635) 201366
12-2.30 (not Tue), 6.30-11; 12-3, 7-10.30 (Sun)
Arkell's 3B; Morland Original; West Berkshire Brick Kiln, Goldstar, seasonal beers Ⓗ
Regional CAMRA pub of the year 1997. Former alehouse for thirsty kiln workers, with three small basic bars and taproom, used by locals and walkers alike. Surrounded only by meadows and forest. Decor and service are both deliberately old-fashioned. A fine rural gem. Filled rolls only Tue and Sun. On the Yattendon to Bucklebury Road: ignore signs to Frilsham. *Recommended.*
♨ Q ❀ ◐ ◑ ♣ P ⚟

Grazeley E3

The areas around Grazeley and Grazeley Green have often been earmarked for a vast new housing estate, but nothing has come of it – yet!

Old Bell
Grazeley Green (OS 683672)
☎ (0118) 988 3115
11-11; 12-10.30 (Sun)
Boddingtons Bitter; Greenalls Original; Young's Special; guest beer Ⓗ
Large bar, restaurant and motel complex. Miller's kitchen with emphasis on Mexican food. Mainly younger clientele. Member of Greenalls' weekly guest beer scheme. Swan necks and sparklers on all beers. Sky Sports TV.

Wheatsheaf
Mereoak Lane (off A33)
☎ (0118) 988 3535
11-11; 12-10.30 (Sun)
Morland Original; Ruddles Best Ⓗ
Brightly polished lounge bar in an attractive-looking rustic cottage building. TV and video. No food Sun–Tue evenings. *Recommended.*
❀ ◐ ◑ P

Great Shefford B2

A pleasant Downland village and home to Butts Brewery. Nearby West Shefford was where Charles I had a camp during the Battle of Newbury.

Swan
Newbury Road (A338)
☎ (01488) 648271
11-2.30, 6.30-11.30; 12-2.30, 7-10.30 (Sun)
Courage Best, Directors; Draught Bass Ⓖ
Originally a coaching inn dating from 1818 and set in the now diminutive village of 'Great' Shefford, this pub backs on to the river Lambourn. Unfortunately, recent internal renovation has lost any character previously present and the emphasis is on rather pricey food.

Halfway B3

Halfway Inn
Bath Road (A4)
☎ (01488) 658215
11.30-2.30, 6-11; 12-3, 7-10.30 (Sun)
Badger Dorset Best, Golden Champion, Tanglefoot; Wadworth 6X Ⓗ
Eighteenth-century oak-beamed pub, decorated with farming implements. Separate restaurant with no-smoking area. Fifty-three miles from Bath and London, hence its name. Meals served lunch and eve every day.
Recommended.
⌂ ❀ ◑ ◐ ⊬

Hampstead Norreys C2

Not so long ago, the village had two pubs, but when Morland bought the White Hart from Whitbread, they duly closed the excellent New Inn – despite intense protests from locals, the press and CAMRA.

White Hart
Church Street
☎ (01635) 202248
11-3,6-11; 11-11 (Sat); 12-10.30 (Sun)
Morland Original; Ruddles Best; guest beer Ⓗ
Large village centre pub with small tiled central bar. Right-hand bar behind large fireplace is dedicated mainly to pool and darts and attracts younger drinkers whereas the left-hand bar is somewhat smarter. Basic menu available 12–2, 7–9.15. Disabled access and toilet. Base for Hampstead Norreys Cricket Club. Board games and table tennis available. Cider on fake handpump.

Hamstead Marshall B4

The river Kennet and the canal form an attractive setting around Hamstead Mill with two bridges, a lock and the weir.

White Hart
Church Street (OS 528763)
☎ (01488) 658201
11-3, 6.30-11; closed Sun
Thomas Hardy Country; Wadworth 6X Ⓗ
Oak-beamed country pub focusing on restaurant standard food with an Italian slant.
Recommended.
⌂ Q ❀ ⛟ ◑ ◐ P

Hare Hatch G2

Horse & Groom
Bath Road (A4)
☎ (0118) 940 3136
11-11; 12-10.30 (Sun)
Boddingtons Bitter; Brakspear Bitter, Special Ⓗ
Standard Beefeater decor although some original features have been retained. Restaurant at rear.

Queen Adelaide
Blakes Lane (off A4)
Closed – future uncertain.

'I envy people who drink. At least they know what to blame everything on'

Oscar Levant

Queen Victoria
The Holt, Blakes Lane (off A4)
☎ (0118) 940 2477
11-2.30 (3 summer), 5.30-11;
12-10.30 (Sun)
Brakspear Bitter, Special, Old, Seasonal Ales Ⓗ
Great food and pleasant surroundings. Several walks pass nearby making the pub a pitstop on the way. Food served until 10 on Sundays. *Recommended.*
❀ ◐◑ ♣ P ⚟

Heath End D4

The main part of the village is in Hampshire.

Falcon
Burghfield Road (A340)
☎ (0118) 981 3756
11-11; 12-10.30 (Sun)
Whitbread Trophy; **Flowers** Original; **Boddingtons** Bitter Ⓗ
Roadside pub with two bars. The small front bar has pool and table football and the larger lounge at the rear contains the food servery. Old brewery-related photos and posters included in the decor. Regular quiz nights, prize bingo and discos. Large garden with children's play area.

Hermitage C3

Fox Inn
Yattendon Road (B4009)
☎ (01635) 201545
11-3, 5.30-11; 11-11 (Wed-Sat);
12-10.30 (Sun)
Courage Best, Directors; **Theakston** XB Ⓗ
Comfortable pub with public bar separated from lounge by partition. Lounge leads to quiet eating area. *Recommended.*
⌂ Q ❀ ◐◑ ⊟ ♿

'A night of good drinking is worth a year's thinking'

Charles Cotton (1630–1687)

Lamb
Long Lane (B4009)
☎ (01635) 200348
12-2.30 (3 Sat), 6 (5.30 Fri)-11;
12-3, 7-10.30 (Sun)
Flowers IPA, Original; **Wadworth** 6X; guest mild Ⓗ
Large brick-fronted pub set back from the road. The single bar is discreetly decorated and still maintains distinct areas within. One of the few pubs in the area regularly serving mild. *Recommended.*
Q ❀ ◐◑ ♿ ♣ P ⚟

White Horse
Newbury Road (B4009)
☎ (01635) 200325
11-2.30 (3 Sat), 6-11; 12-3, 7-10.30 (Sun)
Morland Original, Old Speckled Hen; **Ruddles** Best Ⓗ
Village centre pub with large public bar to left of entrance with quieter, smaller lounge to right. Car park at front. *Recommended.*
Q ❀ ◐◑ ⊟ ♿ ♣ P ⚟

Holyport H2

The village green has been the centre for numerous activities (including international cricket) over the centuries, and has even been used as a film set! Real Tennis is still played at The Lodge and Holyport residents once had a glimpse of the future in the form of the first section of the M4 motorway – started in 1938!

Belgian Arms
Holyport Street
☎ (01628) 634468
11-3, 5.30-11; 12-3, 7-10.30 (Sun)
Brakspear Bitter, Special Ⓗ
Excellent village pub situated near green and pond. Originally called the Eagle but the name was changed during WW1 after German POWs saluted the pub sign as they were marched by. *Recommended.*
⌂ Q ❀ ◐◑ ♿ P

George
The Green
☎ (01628) 628317
11-3, 5-11; 12-3, 7-10.30 (Sun)
Courage Best, Directors; Marston's Pedigree Ⓗ
Pleasant, busy pub overlooking the village green.

Sun & Stars
Forest Green Road
☎ (01628) 623639
12-3, 6-11; 12-5 (Sun)
Morland Original; Ruddles County Ⓗ
Buildings date from 1750. Excellent home-cooked food available most times except Sun eve. Barbecues in the garden on Sun in summer.

Horton J2

The small village green and the ancient squat church contribute to the village's character. The poet Milton lived here in his youth and nearby is The Queen Mother Reservoir – one of the biggest artificial reservoirs in the country.

Crown
Horton Road
☎ (01753) 682407
11-11; 12-10.30 (Sun)
Morland Original; Ruddles Best; guest beer Ⓗ
Pleasant old pub by the village green.

Five Bells
Stanwell Road
☎ (01753) 682193
11-11; 12-10.30 (Sun)
Greene King IPA, Triumph, Abbot Ⓗ
Quiet old pub on the edge of the village. Once owned by Horton church.

Hungerford A3

An attractive historic market town at the tributary of the river Kennet, Dun and Kennet & Avon Canal. Renowned trout fishing after John of Gaunt granted fishing rights in the 14th century. The annual Hocktide celebrations take place on the second Tuesday after Easter, marking the day by which all rents and fines were due to be paid. Two Tutti-men accompany the Orangeman to collect rent (or a kiss nowadays) from houses that retain commoners rights. An Ale-Tasting ceremony rounds off the week ensuring that the town continues to serve 'a goodly brew'!

Bear Hotel
Charnham Street (A4)
☎ (01488) 682512
11-11, 12-10.30 (Sun)
Draught Bass; Hancock's HB Ⓗ
Old coaching inn with a history that can be traced to the 13th century. Four star accommodation.

Borough Arms
77 High Street (A338)
☎ (01488) 683233
11-3, 6-11; 12-3, 6-10.30 (Sun)
Wadworth Henry's IPA, 6X, Farmer's Glory Ⓗ
Extensive L-shaped bar catering mainly for locals. Large screen TV for major sporting events. *Recommended.*
❀ ◐◑ ⇌

Downgate
13 Down View, Park Street
☎ (01488) 682708
11-2.30, 6-11; 12-3, 7-10.30 (Sun)
Arkell's 3B Ⓗ
Small community local with no fancy gimmicks which looks out over the famous common and attracts dog walkers and other visitors. Popular Sunday roast. Lunches need advance booking. *Recommended.*
🏰 Q ❀ ◐◑ ⇌ ♣ P

Hungerford Club
3 The Croft (off Church Street)
☎ (01488) 682358
12-3 (not Mon-Fri), 7-11 (10.30 Sun)
Morland Original; Ruddles Best; guest beer Ⓗ
Sports and social club overlooking the croft green where tennis and bowls are played in the summer. Reasonably priced beer including regularly changing guest ale. Show this Guide or CAMRA membership card to be signed in! *Recommended.*
❀ ⇌ ♣ P

John O'Gaunt
Bridge Street (A338)
☎ (01488) 683535
11-11; 12-10.30 (Sun)
Morland Independent IPA, Original; **Ruddles** County Ⓗ
Sixteenth-century building but did not become a pub until 1780. John o' Gaunt ruled England as viceroy for the senile Edward III in the 14th century. Morland managed pub offering accommodation and pub grub.

Just William
50 Church Street
☎ (01488) 681199
11-3, 5.30-11; 12-3, 6.30-10.30 (Sun)
Brakspear Bitter; **Fuller's** London Pride Ⓗ
Comfortable bar within a restaurant. Has changed names several times since originally known as the Angel.

Lamb
5 Charnham Street (A4)
☎ (01488) 686390
11-3, 6-11; 12-3, 7-10.30 (Sun)
Ushers Best, Founders, occasional seasonal beers Ⓗ
Pub/restaurant serving good quality home-cooked food in comfortable surroundings; lounge features real fire and armchairs. Single rooms B&B available. *Recommended.*
Q ❀ ◖◗ ⇄ P

Lion
Charnham Street (A4)
☎ (01488) 682588
11-3, 6-11; 12-3, 7-10.30 (Sun)
Courage Best; **Theakston** XB Ⓗ
Roadside pub, parts of which date back 500 years. For many years known as the Red Lion but has laboured under several names since.

Plume
113 High Street
☎ (01488) 682154
11-3, 6-11; 12-3, 7-10.30 (Sun)
Morland Original, Old Speckled Hen Ⓗ
Town centre pub popular with the younger crowd.

Railway
Station Road (near A338)
☎ (01488) 683100
11-11; 12-10.30 (Sun)
Hook Norton Bitter; **Fuller's** London Pride; guest beers Ⓗ
A recent major refurbishment created a small front bar that opens into a larger concert hall where a variety of rock bands draw the weekend crowds. Pleasant patio and large garden. The pub is near enough to the station to call one bar 'Platform Three'. *Recommended.*
❀ ◖◗ ⇄ ♣

Sun Inn
36 Charnham Street (A4)
☎ (01488) 682162
11.30-11; 12-10.30 (Sun)
Morland Original; **Draught Bass** Ⓗ
Homely, one-bar pub with separate dining room. Entertainment includes pool and darts. Evening meals on request. Patio area. Accommodation: two rooms en suite. *Recommended.*
❀ ◖◗ ⇄ ♣ P

Three Swans Hotel
117 High Street
☎ (01488) 682721
11-11; 12-10.30 (Sun)
Courage Best, Directors; **Theakstons** XB Ⓗ
Hotel bar popular with young people especially at weekends.

Hungerford Newtown A3

Tally-Ho
(A338, three miles north of Hungerford)
☎ (01488) 682312
11-3, 6-11; 11-11 (Sat); 12-10.30 (Sun)
Wadworth IPA, 6X Ⓗ
Unpretentious two-bar pub with small dining room. Situated on dangerous 'blind' crossroads – great care needed when arriving and departing! *Recommended.*
Q ❀ ◖◗ P

Hurley G1

A delightful riverside village with an ancient priory and some very picturesque backwaters.

Black Boy
Henley Road (A423)
☎ (01628) 824212
11.30–2.30 (3 Sat), 6–11; 12–3, 7–10.30 (Sun)
Brakspear Mild, Bitter Ⓗ
Basic old, no-frills pub, but none the worse for that. Ideal for a quiet pint. *Recommended.*

Dew Drop Inn
Batts Green, Honey Lane (off A423, OS 824815)
☎ (01628) 824327
12–3, 6–11; 12–3, 7–10.30 (Sun)
Brakspear Bitter, Special, seasonal beers Ⓗ
Small old pub with large garden. Not the easiest place to find but well worth the effort. Good place to recover following a walk in surrounding Ashley Hill woods. *Recommended.*

East Arms
Henley Road (A423)
☎ (01628) 823227
11–11; 12–10.30 (Sun)
Boddingtons Bitter; Greenalls Original; guest beer Ⓗ
Large and comfortable 'Miller's Kitchen' pub with 'Adventure Island' children's play room. Good play area in garden as well. Food available throughout the day.

Old Bell
High Street
No Real Ale.

Red Lion
Applehouse Hill, Henley Road (near A423)
☎ (01628) 824433
11–3, 6–11; 12–3, 7–10.30 (Sun)
Brakspear Bitter; Draught Bass Ⓗ
Friendly 18th-century coaching inn. The listed cellar is built over the original cellar which dates back to the Domesday Book. *Recommended.*

Rising Sun
High Street
☎ (01628) 824274
11.30–3, 5.30–11.30; 12–3.30, 7–10.30 (Sun)
Brakspear Bitter; Fuller's London Pride Ⓗ
Two-bar pub dating back to Tudor times. Flagstone floor in front bar, low beams in both. Rear extension planned. (Open all day in summer.) *Recommended.*

Hurst G3

Nearby is Dinton Pastures Country Park.

Castle
Church Hill (off B3030)
☎ (0118) 934 0034
Opening varies; closed Mon eve
Ruddles Best; Marston's Pedigree; Morland Old Speckled Hen Ⓗ
Former pub now a restaurant with small bar. Drinks pricey.

Elephant & Castle
Lodge Road (B3030)
☎ (0118) 934 0886
11–3.30, 5.30–11; 11–11 (Fri, Sat); 12–10.30 (Sun)
Morland Original; Ruddles County; guest beer Ⓗ
Country pub with neat lounge containing small dining area and larger, more lively public bar specialising in pub games. Bar billiards, darts and cards played. Guest beer is pricey.

Green Man
Hinton Road (off A321)
☎ (0118) 934 2599
11.30–2.30, 6–11; 12–2.30, 6–10.30 (Sun) (longer opening in Summer)
Brakspear Bitter, Special, seasonal beers Ⓗ
Superb 17th-century village pub with several small bars to explore. Emphasis on food which is good quality and reasonably priced but nonetheless, still a beer-drinkers' pub. Separate no-smoking dining area. Disabled toilet. *Recommended.*

Jolly Farmer

Davis Street (B3030)
☎ (0118) 934 1881
12-3, 5.30-11; 12-11 (Sat); 12-10.30 (Sun)
Morland Original; **Ruddles** County; Draught **Bass** Ⓗ
Lively, two-bar locals' pub. Wooden floor in public bar; bright white walls all round. Interesting 19th-century auction documents displayed on wall. Say hello to Oscar the parrot. Darts team. Garden with children's play area.

Inkpen A4

An unusually named village which is considered to be the start of the Wansdyke Way and features a rare preserved gibbet at nearby Inkpen Beacon, from which fine views can be obtained over the chalk downs.

Crown & Garter

Great Common, Inkpen Common
☎ (01488) 668325
12-3, 6.30-11; 12-3, 6.30-10.30 (Sun)
Archers Village, Golden; **West Berkshire** Good Old Boy Ⓗ
Thriving village local serving well kept locally produced ales. Excellent home-cooked food with generous portions. Closed all day Mon and Tue lunch. B&B planned. *Recommended.*

Swan

Craven Road, Lower Green (OS 359643)
☎ (01488) 668326
11-3, 7-11; 12-3, 7-10.30 (Sun); closed (Mon, Tue)
Hook Norton Mild, Bitter; **Butts** Bitter, seasonal beers Ⓗ
New owners in 1996 are slowly and steadily rebuilding and refurbishing in style sympathetic to this 16th-century country pub. Accommodation suite of ten rooms added. Includes organic food shop, while menu is mainly organic. Real cider from Lambourn Valley. *Recommended.*

Kintbury B3

A small town or a large village? Either way Kintbury is a very pleasant Kennet Valley community which is popular with anglers. There is a fine old mill (now converted to flats) and a picturesque parish church. The railway and the canal run side-by-side through the area and the station is right by the Dundas Arms.

Blue Ball

High Street
☎ (01488) 608126
11-11; 12-10.30 (Sun)
Courage Best Ⓗ
Two-bar pub offering pool and darts.

Green Man, Hurst

Dundas Arms Hotel
Station Road (OS 386672)
☎ (01488) 658263
11-2.30, 6-11; 12-2.30, 6-10.30 (Sun)
Ringwood Best; **Morland** Original; **Charles Wells** Bombardier Ⓗ
Canalside pub with white-washed exterior, near Kintbury station. Look for bar counter which is studded with polished old pennies. No food Sun. *Recommended.*
Q ❀ 🛏 ◖◗ ⇌ P

Prince of Wales
Newbury Street
☎ NOT LISTED
11-3, 6-11; 11-11 (Sat); 12-3, 7-10.30 (Sun)
Tetley Bitter Ⓗ
Old, tile-clad fronted pub in centre of village, serving the local population.

Knowl Hill G2

Originally a Roman settlement and latterly named after a clump of trees (knoll of Elms) which had stood in the area since 1315. There are remnants of the large brick-making industry which stood alongside the busy A4 road; and during the second weekend in August, the village plays host to the country's second largest steam rally and fair.

Bird in Hand
Bath Road (A4)
☎ (01628) 826622/822781
11-3, 6-11; 12-3, 7-10.30 (Sun)
Brakspear Bitter, seasonal beers; **Fuller's** London Pride Ⓗ
Splendid 14th-century inn which is also a genuine free house and has been in the same family for three generations. The Oak Lounge has a baronial ambience. Pictures of steam traction engines reflect Knowl Hill's status as a Steam Rally venue. Food served at all times (finishes 2.30 lunchtime). Accommodation includes one bedroom for disabled. Conference facilities for up to 15 people. *Recommended.*
🜲 Q ❀ 🛏 ◖◗ ♿ P

Old Devil
Bath Road (A4)
☎ (01628) 822764
11-11; 12-10.30 (Sun)
Badger IPA, Dorset Best, Tanglefoot, seasonal beers Ⓗ
Comfortable roadside pub with several distinct drinking areas including large side bar with TV. Good menu (food until 10 every night). Nice rear garden with children's play area. B&B. Coaches welcome in large car park. *Recommended.*
❀ 🛏 ◖◗ P

Royal Oak
(just off A4)
☎ (01628) 822010
12-3, 5-11; 12-3 (Sun)
Brakspear Bitter; **Adnams** Extra Ⓗ
One-time country pub, now a small restaurant with bar and seating area. Closed Sun eve and all day Mon.

Seven Stars
Bath Road (A4)
☎ (01628) 822967
11-11; 12-10.30 (Sun)
Brakspear Bitter, Special, seasonal beers Ⓗ
Fine old inn which, despite conversion into one large bar, still retains much character including a lot of wood panelling. Separate games room. Quoits and darts. *Recommended.*
🜲 ❀ ◖◗ ♣ P

Lambourn A2

Situated on the river of the same name, Lambourn is a well-known horse racing centre with several stables and gallops. There are also many ancient burial sites in the area, including the Seven Barrows.

George Hotel
High Street (B4001)
☎ (01488) 71889
11-3, 6-11; 12-3, 7-10.30 (Sun)
Arkell's 3B Ⓗ
Village centre pub; very welcoming to visitors. Walls adorned with racing bric-a-brac. Food lunchtimes only. *Recommended.*
❀ 🛏 ◖ ♣ P

Lamb Inn
46 Newbury Street
☎ (01488) 71552
Opening hours unavailable
Courage Best Ⓗ
Town-style pub with a lounge and public bar. The public bar appears to suit locals whilst visitors generally use the lounge. Riverside garden.

Malt Shovel
Malt Shovel Lane, Upper Lambourn
☎ (01488) 71623
11-3, 6-11; 12-3, 7-10.30 (Sun)
Hampshire King Alfred; guest beer Ⓗ
Unpretentious village local in the heart of the racing community. Popular with walkers. Lunchtime and evening meals Mon–Sat. *Recommended.*
❀ ◖◗ ⊟ ♣

Valentines
High Street
No Real Ale.

Wheelwright Arms
4 The Broadway
☎ (01488) 71643
12-11; 12-10.30 (Sun)
Morland Original Ⓗ
Three-room pub near the village square, popular with local stable lads.

Lambourn Woodlands A2

Hare & Hounds
(B4000, OS 317759)
☎ (01488) 71386
11-3, 7-11; 12-3, 7-10.30 (Sun)
Wadworth 6X; Flowers IPA Ⓗ
Pleasing 18th-century country pub on main road. A friendly welcome is extended to locals and strangers alike. Tastefully decorated, this pub caters for all.

Langley J2

A residential suburb to the east of Slough.

Arkle
High Street
No Real Ale.

Chestnuts
St Marys Road
☎ (01753) 544237
11-11; 12-10.30 (Sun)
Courage Best, Directors Ⓗ
Community local where darts and pool feature highly. Juke box also well used. Irish landlord ensures a Gaelic atmosphere. *Recommended.*
❀ ◖◗ ⊟ ♿ ♣ P

Harrow
290 High Street
☎ (01753) 543700
No Real Ale but likely to change.

Merrymakers
Meadow Road
☎ (01753) 594894
11-11; 12-10.30 (Sun)
Greene King IPA, Martha Greene; guest beer Ⓗ
Hungry Horse eating house popular with families. Separate sports bar with large screen TV. Can get very lively.

Montagu Arms
374 London Road (A4)
☎ (01753) 543009
12-11; 12-10.30 (Sun)
Draught Bass; M&B Brew XI Ⓗ
Harvester restaurant and family pub near M4 junction 5. *Recommended.*
❀ ◖◗ P

Murphy's
Parlaunt Road
No Real Ale.

> 'A fine beer may be judged with just one sip, but it is better to be thoroughly sure'
>
> *Anon*

Red Lion
1 St Mary's Road
☎ (01753) 582235
11-11; 12-10.30 (Sun)
Greene King IPA, Martha Greene, Abbot; **Courage** Best; guest beer Ⓗ
Recently refurbished traditional pub with some original Tudor features. The fireplace is worth a visit in its own right. Near church and almshouses in historic part of Langley. *Recommended.*

Toby Carvery
London Road (A4)
☎ (01753) 591212
11-11; 12-10.30 (Sun)
Draught **Bass; Stones** Bitter Ⓗ
Previously the William IV, the name was changed during recent refurbishment. Emphasis on food. Motel style accommodation. Close to M4 junction 5.

Willow Tree
62 Station Road
☎ (01753) 811336/811491
11-11; 12-10.30 (Sun)
Courage Best, Directors; **Fuller's** London Pride; **Marston's** Pedigree; **John Smith's** Bitter Ⓗ
Locals' pub by Langley station with willow tree in the beer garden. Regular live music. Sun quiz night. Popular at lunchtimes with workers from nearby industrial estate. *Recommended.*

Leckhampstead B2

Stag
Shop Lane
☎ (01488) 638436
7-11; 12-2.30, 7-11 (Thur-Sat); 12-2.30, 7-10.30 (Sun)
Morland Original; **Wadworth** 6X Ⓗ
One-room village local with dining and games areas. Interesting old photos of village life. Food until 9 (good but not cheap). Closed Mon–Wed lunchtimes.

Little Sandhurst G4

Bird in Hand
High Street (near A321)
☎ (01344) 772459
11-3, 5.30-11; 11-11 (Sat); 12-10.30 (Sun)
Morland Original, Tanner's Jack; **Ruddles** County; guest beer Ⓗ
Welcoming and unspoilt classic two-bar 1930s pub with landlord keen on real ale. Large patio and garden. No food Sun eve. *Recommended.*

Fox & Hounds
Hancombe Road (off High Street, OS 832626)
☎ (01344) 772765
11-3, 6-11; 11-11 (Sat); 12-10.30 (Sun)
Greene King IPA Ⓗ
Hidden down potholed lane on edge of woods. Split lounge with games room. Large garden.

Littlewick Green G2

The village green (just off the A4) doubles as a cricket pitch and was often used in old British films. The church is worth a visit for its remarkable reredos – an early Quattrocentro painting of the Adoration of the Magi.

Cricketers
Coronation Road (off A4)
☎ (01628) 822888
11-11; 12-10.30 (Sun)
Brakspear Bitter; **Fuller's** London Pride; **Timothy Taylor** Landlord; guest beer Ⓗ
Freehouse overlooking cricket pitch on eponymous green. Home-cooked food available lunchtimes and evenings. Good value accommodation; handy for nearby business park. *Recommended.*

Crown, Lower Basildon

Riders Country House Hotel
Bath Road (A4)
☎ (01628) 822085
10-12; closed Sun
Ruddles Best Ⓗ
Intimate country house hotel, restaurant and bar. Once owned by Freddie Starr.

Ring O' Bells
Bath Road (A4)
☎ (01628) 825987
12-11; 12-10.30 (Sun)
Thomas Greenall's Original; Worthington Draught Ⓗ
Large roadside pub now converted into smart restaurant with relaxed atmosphere. Food orders until 10 (9 Sun). Occasional live music. Disabled access and toilet. Previously known as 'Bell & Bottle'.

Shire Horse
Maidenhead Thicket, Bath Road (A4)
☎ (01628) 825335
11-11; 12-10.30 (Sun)
Courage Best Ⓗ
Large pub on the A4 next to the Shire Horse Centre, visitors from which make up most of the trade.

Lower Basildon D2

Jethro Tull – the agricultural innovator, not the rock band – was born here. Nearby is Basildon Park (NT) house and gardens.

Crown
Reading Road (A329)
☎ (01491) 671262
11-3, 6-11; 12-3, 6-10.30 (Sun)
Morland Original; Ruddles Best Ⓗ
Once known as 'Old Mary's Inn' after a previous landlady who refurbished the pub as a result of trade from navvies who were building Brunel's Great Western Railway. Formerly several rooms, now opened out into one comfortable open-plan bar plus no-smoking restaurant. Views across the Thames Valley to the Chilterns. Bar billiards. *Recommended.*

Lower Earley F3

A vast new housing estate south of Reading (see also Earley).

Culpeper Mill
2 The Square, Chalfont Way
☎ (0118) 975 0381
11-11; 12-10.30 (Sun)
Draught Bass; Hancock's HB; Stones Bitter; Worthington Draught; guest beer Ⓗ
Open-plan family pub/diner, divided into discrete areas. Popular with families with children. All beers served through swan necks, tight sparklers and too cold. Food most times.

Earley Retreat
Chalfont Place, Elm Lane
☎ (0118) 923 0251
11-11; 12-10.30 (Sun)
Draught Bass; Fuller's London Pride Ⓗ
Modern open-plan sports bar in centre of shopping precinct. Mainly younger clientele. Family area open until 8. Large-screen TV.

Seven Red Roses
19 Maiden Place
☎ (0118) 935 9551
11-11; 12-10.30 (Sun)
Draught Bass; Fuller's London Pride Ⓗ
Formulaic modern bar in housing estate. Flagged floor, TV projector and good beer. No food Wed eve. The name came from a competition to find a new pub name.

Maidenhead H2

The centre of this riverside town is an odd mixture of old and new, with the large shopping precinct being the former site of Nicholson's Brewery (which closed in 1960 and whose slogan was 'Best in the Long Run'). The areas alongside the Thames are worth exploring, with the beautifully balustraded Maidenhead Bridge being a fine example of Georgian masonry and Brunel's railway viaduct reputedly having the world's largest brick span. Upstream is Boulter's Lock with the woods of Cliveden beyond (well worth a visit). As far as the beer is concerned, the town has mainly been dominated by Courage although there are a few other brewers represented and there are still some good old-fashioned pubs left in the area.

Anchor
33 York Road
No Real Ale.

'If die I must, let me die drinking in an inn'

Walter Map (1140–1209)

Ark ❶
20 Ray Street
☎ (01628) 418707
12-11; 12-10.30 (Sun)
Courage Best Ⓗ
Comfortable two-bar local near the Thames, hence the name. Separate pool room. Occasional quiz nights, karaoke etc for charity.

Bear ❷
8–10 High Street
☎ (01628) 625183
12-11; 12-12 (Thur-Sat); 12-10.30 (Sun)
Boddington Bitter; Worthington Best Ⓗ
Large two-floor pub which is the major youth venue in town.

Bell
95 King Street
No Real Ale.

Boulters Lock Inn/Hotel
Boulters Island
No Real Ale.

Brewers ❸
105 High Street
☎ (01628) 622830
11-11; 12-10.30 (Sun)
Courage Best, Directors; guest beers Ⓗ
Large pub at the end of the High Street, close to the bus terminus and market. Live music winter weekends. Small patio area at side. A dispute with the local council about having to use plastic glasses means that the pavement drinking area may not survive. *Recommended.*
❀ ◑ ⇄

Chicago Rock Café
Queen Street
No Real Ale.

Craufurd Arms ❹
15 Gringer Hill (A308)
☎ (01628) 625153
11.30-2.30, 5-11; 12-3, 7-10.30 (Sun)
Flowers IPA Ⓗ
Small one-bar pub with small car park. Food available lunchtimes. Dartboard.

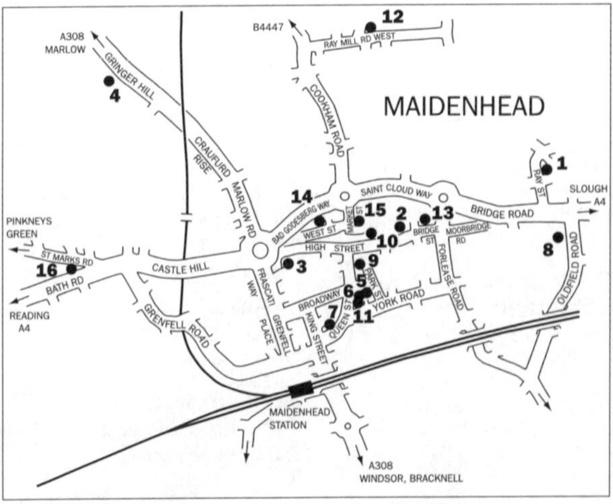

Cricketers Arms ❺

18 Park Street
☎ (01628) 638332
11-11; 12-10.30 (Sun)
Morland Independent IPA, Original Ⓗ
The original bar is now the pool bar, while the extension, built in the 80s, is now the main trading area. Locals' pub with satellite TV for sports and live music Fri and Sat nights. A touch Irish but not overwhelmingly so. Renovations summer 1999. Public car park (pay) opposite.

Crooked Billet

34 Westborough Road (off A4)
☎ (01628) 622727
11-11; 12-10.30 (Sun)
Courage Best; guest beer Ⓗ
Locals' pub to the west of town centre.

Crown

108 Wootton Way (off A4)
☎ (01628) 622897
11-11; 12-10.30 (Sun)
Courage Best; Brakspear Special Ⓗ
Large two-bar pub by railway bridge at the foot of Boyn Hill. Food available from 12–9.30.

Custom House

90 Moorbridge Road
No Real Ale.

Farmer's Boy

2 Harrow Lane (jnct B4447)
☎ (01628) 623033
11-11; 12-10.30 (Sun)
Draught Bass; Greene King IPA, Abbot, Triumph; John Smith's Bitter; guest beer Ⓗ
Pub with a fishing theme, a short distance from Furze Platt station. Food available every day. *Recommended.*
⛫ ❀ ◐◑ ⇌ P

Finnegan's Wake ❻

43 Queen Street
☎ (01628) 634740
11-11; 12-10.30 (Sun)
Courage Best Ⓗ
Irish theme pub with wine bar pretensions. Pavement drinking area.

Fir Cone

53 Norreys Drive
☎ (01628) 631159
11-11; 12-10.30 (Sun)
Courage Best; guest beer Ⓗ
Pub situated on the edge of Larchfield Estate.

'Best while you have it use your breath, there is no drinking after death'

John Fletcher (1579–1625)

Flood & Firkin ❼
Queen Street
☎ NOT LISTED
11-11; 12-10.30 (Sun)
Firkin Best, Flood, Dogbolter Ⓗ
New pub based on familiar Firkin concept opened in 1998. Live music weekends. Food available 12–8.30 every day.

Frederick's Hotel & Restaurant
Shoppenhangers Road
No Real Ale.

Golden Harp
67 Furze Platt Road, Furze Platt (A308)
☎ (01628) 630323
11-11; 12-10.30 (Sun)
Flowers Original Ⓗ
Large suburban pub with central bar and sections around it including a pool room. About one mile north of town centre on Marlow road. Food available until 8.30.

Grenfell Arms ❽
22 Oldfield Road
☎ (01628) 620705
11-11; 12-10.30 (Sun)
Morland Original, Old Speckled Hen Ⓗ
A smallish main bar with two log fires. Recent refurbishment has focused on separate (machine) 'games room'. Next door to Nortel. *Recommended.*
🜲 ❀ ◖ ≉ ♣ P

Hand & Flowers ❾
15 Queen Street
☎ (01628) 623800
11.30-11; 2-10.30 (Sun)
Brakspear Bitter, Special, seasonal beers Ⓗ
A major refurbishment in 1999 has avoided changing the character too much. Real ale is very much a priority in this excellent pub. Note Sunday opening is 2 not 12! *Recommended.*
◖ ≉

Hobgoblin ❿
34 High Street
☎ (01628) 636510
12-11; opening varies-10.30 (Sun)
Wychwood Shires, Special, Hobgoblin, Dog's Bollocks Ⓗ
Large, dimly lit youngsters' pub. Music on all the time. Satellite TV. Sport dictates Sunday afternoon (opening one hour before kick-off).

Holiday Inn
Manor Lane
No Real Ale.

Jack of Both Sides (Tut 'n' Shive) ⓫
81 Queen Street
☎ (01628) 620870
11-11; 12-10.30 (Sun)
Fuller's London Pride; Rebellion IPA Ⓗ
On the young people's circuit of town centre pubs.

Masters Arms ⓬
18 North Town Road
☎ (01628) 788845
11.30-3, 5-11; 11.30-11 (Sat); 12-10.30 (Sun)
Flowers Original; Ruddles Best Ⓗ
One large bar with pool tables and occasional karaoke.

Morrisons
2 Norfolk Road
No Real Ale.

New Inn
1 Farm Road
☎ (01628) 777721
11-11; 12-10.30 (Sun)
Courage Best; Brakspear Special Ⓗ
Estate pub with both saloon and public bars. Set menu of 'sizzling platters' and baps/jacket potatoes offers good value. Pool table.

Newt & Cucumber ⓭
2 Bridge Street
☎ (01628) 620074
12-11; 12-12 (Fri); 7-12 (Sat); closed Sun
Ruddles Best; Morland Old Speckled Hen Ⓗ
Formerly known as Pinkertons

but retains the same youthful clientele.

North Star
Westborough Road
☎ (01628) 622711
11-11; 12-10.30 (Sun)
Courage Best; Fuller's London Pride Ⓗ
Small two-bar local. Snacks available lunchtime and evening. Beer garden planned.

North Star
54 North Town Road
☎ (01628) 633511
11-11; 12-10.30 (Sun)
Flowers IPA; Whitbread Trophy Ⓗ
Small, pleasant pub with neighbourhood atmosphere, named after famous 1830s railway engine. *Recommended.*
❀ ≹

Pond House
53 Bath Road (A4)
☎ (01628) 627178
11-11; 12-10.30 (Sun)
Brakspear Bitter; Flowers Original; Fuller's London Pride; Morland Old Speckled Hen; Wadworth 6X; guest beers Ⓗ
Large modern comfortable community local which has been recently refurbished. One quiet bar while the other contains pool table and TV. Food available lunch and evenings until 8. Outside patio. *Recommended.*
❀ ◐◑ P

Portland Arms ⓮
16 West Street
☎ (01628) 634649
12-2.30, 5.30 (6.30 Sat)-11; 7-10.30 (Sun)
Morland Original; Ruddles Best Ⓗ
Small one-bar town centre pub with function room at back. Home-cooked food lunchtime and evenings until 9.30 (not Sun).

Rose
16 King Street
No Real Ale (shortly to change hands).

Swan Vaults
14 Market Street
No Real Ale (shortly to change hands).

Thames Hotel (River Bar)
Ray Mead Road (A4094)
☎ (01628) 628721
11-11; 12-10.30 (Sun)
Brakspear Bitter; Courage Best, Directors Ⓗ
Near Maidenhead bridge; a popular spot in summer to sit on the patio overlooking the river; or to look at the plants inside, or the fans in the ceiling. *Recommended.*
❀ 🛏 ◐◑ ≹ P

Thames Riviera Hotel (Jerome's Bar)
The Bridge (A4)
☎ (01628) 674057
11-11; 12-10.30 (Sun)
Adnams Broadside Ⓗ
Large bar adjacent to restaurant. Food available at all times in bar except 5–6. Adnams Regatta replaces Broadside in summer. *Recommended.*
❀ 🛏 ◐◑ ♿ ≹ P

Vine ⓯
20 Market Street
☎ (01628) 782112
11-11; 12-10.30 (Sun)
Brakspear Bitter, Special, seasonal beers Ⓗ
Excellent, friendly town centre local with popular following. Good atmosphere and historic exterior. Tables out front. *Recommended.*
❀ ◐◑ ≹

Windsor Castle ⓰
Bath Road (A4)
☎ (01628) 621649
11-11; 12-10.30 (Sun)
Theakston Best; Brakspear Special Ⓗ
Pub whose latest refurbishment includes some interesting local photographs.

Marsh Benham B3

Water Rat
(half-mile from A4 west of Newbury, OS 427675)
☎ (01635) 582017
11-3, 6.30-11; 12-3, 7-10.30 (Sun)
Arkell's 3B; Wadworth 6X Ⓗ
Beautiful thatched building now largely set aside for high quality restaurant dining. Extensive renovations planned.
Recommended.
Q ❀ ◑ P

Midgham D3

Rail travellers should note that Midgham station is nowhere near Midgham but is actually in Woolhampton.

Berkshire Arms
Bath Road (A4)
☎ (0118) 971 4114
11-11; 12-10.30 (Sun)
Greenalls Bitter; Young's Special Ⓗ
Hotel with restaurant dining and children's play facilities.

Coach & Horses
Bath Road (A4)
☎ (0118) 971 3384
11.30-3, 6-11; 12-3, 7-10.30 (Sun)
Fuller's London Pride; Flower's Original; guest beer Ⓗ
Pub with small bar area. Meals served every lunchtime and evening. Smoking and no-smoking dining rooms.
Recommended.
🜲 Q ❀ ◑ P

Moneyrow Green H2

Jolly Gardener
Forest Green Road (B3024)
☎ (01628) 622933
11.30-3, 6-11; 11.30-11 (Fri, Sat); 12-10.30 (Sun)
Theakston Best, XB Ⓗ
Formerly known as the Wheel of Fortune. Recently refurbished by Chef & Brewer food/pub chain.

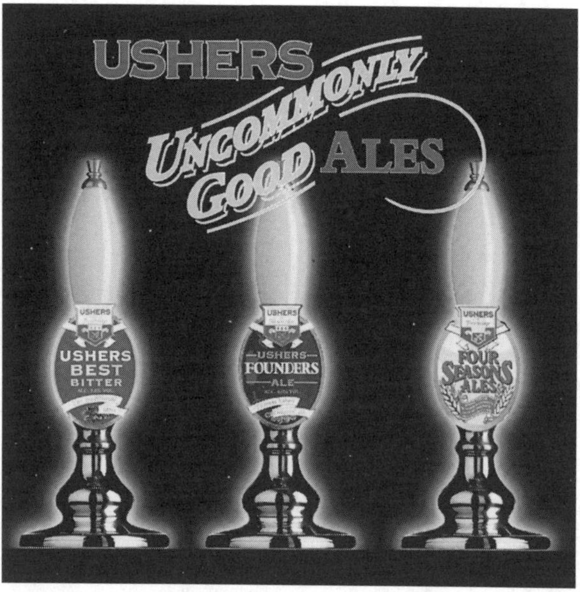

White Hart
(near Holyport)
☎ (01628) 621460
11-11; 12-3, 7-10.30 (Sun)
Morland Original, Old Speckled Hen; Ruddles Best Ⓗ
Unspoilt village local retaining its three bars, built as a hunting lodge for Windsor forest. No noisy electronic distractions in this excellent pub of some charm. *Recommended.*
⛫ Q ❀ ◑ ⊟ ♿ ♣ P

Mortimer E4

Straddles the county boundary with Mortimer West End located in Hampshire.

Carpenters Arms
Windmill Road, Mortimer Common (OS 652647)
☎ (0118) 933 2432
11-11; 12-10.30 (Sun)
Guest beer Ⓗ
Basic but homely backstreet local with no frills. Now a free house but still shows signs of a previous ownership of Blatch's Theale brewery. The one real ale is usually taken from the Greene King seasonal range. Bar billiards.

Fox & Horn
The Street, Stratfield Mortimer
☎ (0118) 933 2428
11-2.30, 5.30-11; 12-2.30, 7-10.30 (Sun)
Young's Bitter; King & Barnes Sussex; Fuller's London Pride; occasional guest beer Ⓗ
Small hotel (four rooms) with pub bar added onto front of original building. Café style tables with friendly service. The name was changed to Railway Hotel when the railway reached the village and has several times alternated between the two names but has now reverted to the original. Function room (for hire) has Wethered's pub signage on display. Separate restaurant.

Horse & Groom
The Street, Mortimer Common
☎ (0118) 933 2813
11-3, 5.30-11; 11-11 (Fri, Sat); 12-10.30 (Sun)
Flowers IPA; Marstons Pedigree, Abbot; Wadworth 6X Ⓗ
Two-bar pub with comfortable lounge (Stirrup's) which is adorned with horse harnesses. The small public bar (Groom's) has a pool table. Handpumps only visible from lounge. Children's menu. Beer range changes in summer.

Turners Arms
West End Road, Mortimer Common
☎ (0118) 933 2961
11.30-2.30 (3 Sat), 5-11; 12-10.30 (Sun)
Brakspear Bitter, Special, seasonal beers Ⓗ
Excellent, efficient one-bar pub which marks the southernmost point of Brakspear's tied estate. The popular restaurant has regular theme evenings (book). The pub was in Hampshire until the county boundaries were changed in the mid-1990s. *Recommended.*
⛫ Q ❀ ◑ ◗ P

Victoria Arms
Victoria Road, Mortimer Common
Real Ale rarely available.

'If all be true that I do
  think,
There are five reasons
  why we drink.
Good wine, friends,
  being dry,
Or that we may be bye
  and bye –
Or any other reason why.'
Anon

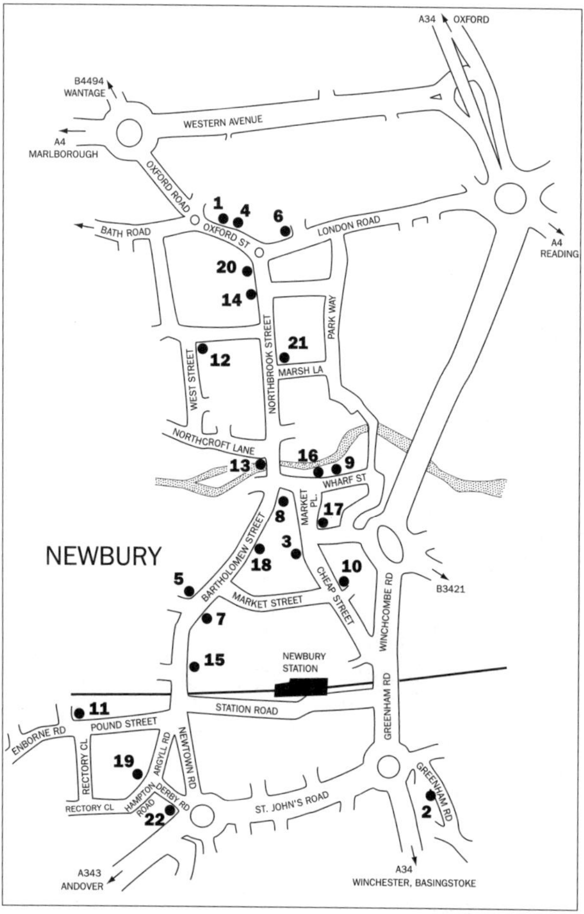

Newbury C3

Although generally known for its racecourse, Newbury is the main commercial and administrative centre of West Berkshire and is home to several hi-tech industries. In the 16th century the town was an important cloth centre where John Winchcombe (nick-named John O'Gaunt) started one of England's first factories, employing over 100 weavers. The old Cloth Hall is now the town museum. During the Civil War, Newbury saw two battles fought just outside the town – a fact commemorated on some of the pub signs.

The Kennet and Avon canal passes through the town and Newbury is a popular stopping-off point for boat crews, not only for provisions but for a beer or two with the town centre offering a good selection of ales from both local and national brewers. The Adnams Brewery – now based in Suffolk – originated in Newbury.

Bacon Arms Hotel ❶

10 Oxford Street
☎ (01635) 31822
11-11; 12-3, 7-10.30 (Sun)
Courage Best, Marston's Pedigree, guest beer Ⓗ
Seventeenth-century town centre pub popular for small business lunches.

Bar Cuba

Saddlers Court,
19 The Broadway
No Real Ale.

Blue Ball ❷
Greenham Road
☎ (01635) 43564
11–11; 12–10.30 (Sun)
Fuller's London Pride; **Ind Coope** Burton Ⓗ
Large public bar with many electronic games, with a quieter lounge and conservatory restaurant. A rare chance to drink Burton Ale in the area. Can be very busy on race days. Large car park. *Recommended.*
❀ ◐ ◑ ⊞ ⇌ P

Catherine Wheel ❸
35 Cheap Street
☎ (01635) 47471
11–11; 12–10.30 (Sun)
Courage Best Ⓗ
Basic town centre pub.

Chequers Hotel ❹
6–8 Oxford Street
☎ (01635) 38000
12–2, 7–11; 12–2, 7–10.30 (Sun)
Flowers Original Ⓔ; **Banks's** Bitter Ⓗ
Hotel with a separate public bar which was originally a coaching inn.

Chicago Rock Café
Cheap Street
No Real Ale.

Coopers Arms ❺
39 Bartholomew Street
☎ (01635) 47469
11–11; 12–10.30 (Sun)
Arkell's 3B Ⓗ
Down-to-earth local with several drinking areas. *Recommended.*
⇌

Cross Keys ❻
8 London Road
☎ (01635) 40101
11–3, 7–11; 11–11 (Sat); 12–10.30 (Sun if football on)
Arkell's 2B Ⓔ, 3B Ⓗ
Town centre pub with main bar and an eating area to the rear. Note Sun opening depends on football – opening may vary if no football on.

Dolphin ❼
113 Bartholomew Street
☎ (01635) 48167
11–11; 12–10.30 (Sun)
Brakspear Bitter, Special; **Courage** Best Ⓗ
Just south of the town, this relatively spacious pub is popular in the evenings. Serves a variety of hot and cold foods.

Hatchet
12 Market Place
No Real Ale.

Hobgoblin ❽
148 Bartholomew Street
☎ (01635) 47336
11–11; 12–10.30 (Sun)
Wychwood Special; **Gales** HSB; **Brakspear** Special; **Wadworth** 6X; **Marston's** Pedigree Ⓗ
One-bar town centre alehouse, decorated in typical basic Hobgoblin style.

Hogshead ❾
1 Wharf Street
☎ (01635) 569895
11–11; 12–10.30 (Sun)
Marston's Pedigree; **Wadworth** 6X; **Boddingtons** Bitter; **Morland** Old Speckled Hen; **Greene King** Abbot; **Fuller's** London Pride Ⓗ
Large converted auction rooms off the Market Place. Serves up to 14 real ales and a selection of imported beers. Outside terrace overlooks canal. Food lunchtimes.

King Charles Tavern ❿
54 Cheap Street
☎ (01635 49127)
11–11; 12–10.30 (Sun)
Morland Original, Old Speckled Hen; Draught **Bass** Ⓗ
Two-bar town pub, one bar of which is air conditioned. Popular collecting place for heavy rock fans.

'You're not drunk if you can lie on the floor without holding on'

Dean Martin

Lamb ⓫
5 Enborne Road
☎ (01635) 40912
11-3, 6-11; 12-3, 7-10.30 (Sun)
Greene King IPA; Brakspear Bitter Ⓗ
True community pub with separate bars offering darts, pool and satellite TV. Needs a facelift inside and out.

Lion ⓬
West Street
☎ (01635) 528468
11-2.30, 5-11; 12-3, 7-10.30 (Sun)
Badger Tanglefoot; Wadworth Henry's IPA, 6X, seasonal beers Ⓗ
Just off the main shopping area, this town centre pub is popular both lunchtimes and evenings. Hot and cold food available. Pool table.

Lock Stock & Barrel ⓭
104 Northbrook Street
☎ (01635) 42730
11-11; 12-10.30 (Sun)
Fuller's London Pride, Chiswick, ESB; seasonal beers Ⓗ
Large one-bar pub just off main shopping street, on the bank of Kennet & Avon canal. Pleasant outdoor drinking areas. *Recommended.*
❀ ◐ ◑ ≉

Monument ⓮
57 Northbrook Street
☎ (01635) 41964
11-11; 12-10.30 (Sun)
Tap & Spile Premium; guest beers Ⓗ
Down-to-earth town pub on main shopping street with partitioned drinking areas. Usually at least four guest beers available, mostly from interesting breweries and Newbury's only regular outlet for the local Butts beers. Recently returned to its original name by popular demand, having been the uninspired 'Tap & Spile' for a short time. *Recommended.*
❀ ◐ ⌂

Nag's Head ⓯
Bartholomew Street
☎ NOT LISTED
11-11; 12-10.30 (Sun)
Courage Best; Wadworth 6X; Marston's Pedigree; Draught Bass Ⓗ
Town centre local with single L-shaped bar.

Newbury Rugby Club
Monks Lane
☎ (01635) 40103
11-11; 12-6 (Sun)
Wadworth 6X; Fuller's London Pride Ⓗ
Set in 35 acres with five rugby pitches, Kicker's Bar & Grill is open to the public. Two further bars available for functions, conferences, etc. Lunches every day and eve meals every day except Sun.

Old London Apprentice
Hambridge Road
☎ (01635) 41483
11-11; 12-10.30 (Sun)
Courage Best; John Smith's Bitter; guest beers Ⓗ
Large, well-furnished lounge with separate games and pool room. Workers on the nearby industrial estate take advantage of the good value meals and home-cooked curries. Can be very busy on race days. Jukebox is often played very loud. Nearest rail station: Newbury Racecourse. *Recommended.*
❀ ◐ ◑ ≉ P

Old Waggon & Horses ⓰
26 Market Place
☎ (01635) 46368
11-11; 12-10.30 (Sun)
Courage Best Ⓗ
One of many pubs in the market place. It is fairly small and access can be difficult as the entrance is on steep steps from the market place.

'One more drink and I'll be under the host!'

Dorothy Parker

Plough on the Green
Greenham Road, Stroud Green
☎ (01635) 38808
12–11; 12–10.30 (Sun)
Courage Best; Draught Bass; Thomas Hardy Royal Oak Ⓗ
Charming old pub opposite Stroud Green, adjacent to Newbury racecourse. Recently extended dining area. Lovely gardens. Lunchtime meals every day. Eve meals Tue–Sat. *Recommended.*
Q ❀ ◐ ◑ ♿ ⇌ P

Queens Hotel ⓱
8 Market Place
☎ (01635) 47447
11–11; 12–3, 7–10.30 (Sun)
Eldridge Pope Royal Oak; Courage Best; Draught Bass Ⓗ
Traditional 19th-century coaching inn located on market square. Features real ale, food and 'olde style' accommodation. Convenient for nearby Corn Exchange arts centre. Extensive lounge area. *Recommended.*
Q ◐ ◑ ⇌ P

Rat & Parrot ⓲
137 Bartholomew Street
☎ (01635) 43254
11–11; 12–10.30 (Sun)
Courage Best Ⓗ
Town pub given a silly gimmicky name to make it sound more trendy. Hopefully it will soon be restored to its proper name, the Bricklayers Arms.

Red House ⓳
12 Hampton Road
☎ (01635) 30584
12–2.30 (3 Sat), 6–11; 12–3, 6–10.30 (Sun)
Marston's Pedigree; guest beer Ⓗ
Comfortably cavernous backstreet boozer, popular with darts, pool and football teams. The landlord loves his television! One of the very few free houses in Newbury. *Recommended.*
⇌ ♣

Rising Sun
Bear Lane
No Real Ale.

Shenanigans ⓴
15 The Broadway
☎ (01635) 43915
11–3, 5–11; 11–11 (Fri, Sat); 12–3, 7–10.30 (Sun)
Courage Best; Wadworth 6X Ⓗ
Formerly the Clocktower, now converted into an 'Oirish' theme bar, although this one is more subtle than many.

Swan
236 London Road (A4)
☎ (01635) 517920/1
11–3, 5.30–11; 12–3, 7–10.30 (Sun)
Draught Bass; Fuller's London Pride Ⓗ
One-bar pub with partitioned areas for dining, games machines and locals! Function room available for hire. No-smoking area. Standard pub fare.

Uncle Henry's ㉑
25 Northbrook Street
☎ (01635) 523249
11–3, 7–11; 12–3, 7–10.30 (Sun)
Courage Best, Directors; Marston's Pedigree Ⓖ
Small pub situated down a walkway off the main shopping street. Beer served by gravity from cooled 'cellar' in room above. Formerly the Castle and other names.

Wellington Arms ㉒
4 Andover Road
☎ (01635) 40117
11–11; 12–10.30 (Sun)
Marston's Pedigree Ⓗ
Attractive brick façade on this small one-bar pub serving local clientele.

White House
London Road (A4)
☎ (01635) 42614
11–11; 12–10.30 (Sun)
Theakston Best, XB; guest beers Ⓗ
Large one-bar community pub with regular entertainment.

Oxford Blue, Old Windsor

North Street E3

Tiny hamlet to the north of Theale.

Thatcher's Arms
(OS 637726)
☎ (0118) 930 2070
12-2.30, 6-11; 12-2.30, 7-10.30 (Sun)
Brakspear Bitter; **Fuller's** London Pride; **Wadworth** 6X Ⓗ
Hard-to-find two-room village pub down winding lanes. Impressive menu but food does not dominate. Food 7–9.30 every day. Bar billiards. Under new management.

Oakley Green H2

Nag's Head
Dedworth Road (B3024)
☎ (01753) 864294
11-11; 12-10.30 (Sun)
Greene King IPA, Abbot; guest beer Ⓗ
A 'Hungry Horse' pub with large children's area situated in pleasant country location. Good for families. Swings and slides in garden. Food available 12–10 (9.30 Sun). Children's menu.

Olde Red Lion
Oakley Green Road (B3024)
☎ (01753) 863892/622722
12-3, 5.30-11; 12-10.30 (Sun)
Draught **Bass**; **Flowers** IPA; **Marston's** Pedigree; **Tetley** Bitter Ⓗ
Four-hundred-year-old coaching inn. Large restaurant provides an extensive menu. Food lunch and eve (12–5 Sun). *Recommended.*
Q❀◐◑P

Old Windsor J3

Although this Thames-side village has few noteworthy buildings today, it is not misnamed, for back in Saxon times – long before the Normans built Windsor Castle – the township here included a royal palace, built by Edward the Confessor. Nearby is Runnymede, where King John signed the Magna Carta in 1215 and where the John F. Kennedy memorial is sited.

Bells of Ouzeley
Straight Road (A308)
☎ (01753) 861526
11-11; 12-10.30 (Sun)
Draught **Bass** Ⓗ
Harvester steakhouse close to the Thames. Handy for walks to Runnymede and JFK memorial. The name is a corruption of Osney, whose abbey had a famous ring of bells. Pub food 11–11. Restaurant 12–12.

Fox & Castle
21 Burfield Road (B3021)
☎ (01753) 832408
11-11; 12-10.30 (Sun)
Courage Best; guest beers Ⓗ
Five-hundred-year-old pub with plush seating one end and pool table the other. Food 12–6

weekdays, all day Sun. Usually two guest beers available. *Recommended.*
❀◐◑P

Jolly Gardeners
92 St Lukes Road (B3021)
☎ (01753) 740893
11–11; 12–10.30 (Sun)
Courage Best; **Ushers** Best, Founders Ⓗ
Single horseshoe-shaped bar with public and saloon bar feel either end. Genuinely friendly community local. Beer range likely to vary. *Recommended.*
❀♣P

Lord Nelson
4 Datchet Road (B3021)
☎ (01753) 858746
12–11; 12–10.30 (Sun)
Ruddles Best Ⓗ
Small one-bar pub on the edge of Home Park. Occasional live music. Quiz night Tue.

Oxford Blue
10 Crimp Hill
☎ (01753) 861954
11–11; 12–10.30 (Sun)
Fuller's London Pride; **Young's** Bitter; **Tetley** Bitter Ⓗ
Lovely old pub, full of character with an aviation theme. Two distinctive bar areas with family room and restaurant. Good reputation for food. Accommodation (five rooms, all en suite). Bar billiards. *Recommended.*
❀◐◑♣P

Union Inn
17 Crimp Hill
☎ (01753) 861955
11–11; 12–10.30 (Sun)
Greene King IPA, Abbot; **Fuller's** London Pride Ⓗ
Old, one-bar pub with restaurant at one end.

Wheatsheaf
Straight Road (A308)
☎ (01753) 860769
11–11; 12–10.30 (Sun)
Tetley Bitter; **Marston's** Pedigree Ⓗ
Large family steakhouse set back from the road with 'Wacky Warehouse' for the children. Restaurant opens at 12.

Padworth Common E3

The Norman church has an impressive chancel arch and the remains of a medieval wall painting.

Round Oak
Burghfield Road
☎ (0118) 970 0365
12–2.30, 6.30–11; 12–10.30 (Sun)
Butts Jester; **Flowers** Original; **Wadworth** 6X Ⓗ
Two distinctly different bars. Cosy panelled lounge with varied furniture and smoky public bar with pool and TV. No food Sun eve. *Recommended.*
❀◐◑P

Round Oak, Padworth Common

Paley Street H2

Bridge House
(B3024)
☎ (01628) 623288
11-11; 12-10.30 (Sun)
Brakspear Bitter; **Flowers** Original; guest beers Ⓗ
Low-beamed pub whose fireplace is decorated with hammers! Guest beers change weekly. No-smoking food area. Refurbishment planned to improve disabled access. *Recommended.*

Royal Oak
(B3024)
☎ (01628) 620541
11.30-3, 5-11; 11.30-11 (Sat); 12-10.30 (Sun)
Fuller's London Pride, ESB, seasonal beers Ⓗ
Old English country pub whose landlord is a master cellarman who takes a delight in looking after his beer. *Recommended.*
Q P

Pangbourne E2

The village takes its name from the River Pang – a local trout stream – and was once home to Kenneth Grahame who wrote *The Wind in the Willows*. Another literary connection is with Jerome K. Jerome whose *Three Men in a Boat* finished their journey at the weir by The Swan.

Road travellers heading into Oxfordshire will have to pay a toll to cross the Thames. Rail travellers have a regular service to Reading, Oxford and London.

'Back and side go bare, go bare, Both foot and hand go cold;
But, belly, God send thee ale enough, Whether it be new or old'

Walter Stevenson (1530–1575)

Copper Inn
Church Road (A340)
☎ (0118) 984 2244
11-3, 5-11; 11-11 (Fri, Sat); 12-10.30 (Sun)
Morland Original; guest beers Ⓗ
Smart lounge bar attached to 19th-century coaching inn (22 bedrooms) on busy road junction next to old parish church in historic village. Licensed for wedding ceremonies. Conference and private dining facilities available. Small outside terrace. *Recommended.*
Q P

Cross Keys
Church Road (A340)
☎ (0118) 984 3268
11-11; 12-10.30 (Sun)
Morland Independent IPA, Old Speckled Hen; **Ruddles** Best; guest beer Ⓗ
Beautiful little 17th-century listed inn backing on to the River Pang. Comfortable lounge with separate family room and snug. Patio area and pergola at rear. Parking can be difficult. Alterations are planned.

George Hotel
The Square (A329)
☎ (0118) 984 2237
11-11; 12-10.30 (Sun)
West Berkshire Good Old Boy Ⓗ
Village bar fronts a large historic old coaching inn which now specialises in business facilities. On the site of an inn established 700 years ago. Hotel offers conference and exhibition facilities for up to 120 people.

Star Inn
25–27 Reading Road (A329)
☎ (0118) 984 2566
11-11; 12-10.20 (Sun)
Morland Original; **Ruddles** Best Ⓗ
Street corner pub specialising in large screen TV sporting events. Family garden and patio. Occasional live bands with bar extension.

Swan
Shooters Hill (A329)
☎ (0118) 984 4494
11-11; 12-10.20 (Sun)
Morland Original; Old Speckled Hen; Ruddles County Ⓗ
Large, multi-roomed Thames-side pub dating back to 1642, situated on narrow road on edge of village. Outdoor terrace with excellent views of river and weir. Extensive food menu with food available every day from 12 includes carvery Sun lunchtimes. Children allowed in several large drinking/eating areas. Small car park but public parking 200 yards under railway bridge. *Recommended.*
❀ ◐◑ ⇄ P

Peasemore C2

Fox & Hounds
Hill Green Road
☎ (01635) 248252
11.30-2.30, 6.30-11; 12-3, 7-10.30 (Sun); closed Mon except Bank Hols
Greene King IPA, Abbot; Marston's Pedigree Ⓗ
Comfortable pub in rural setting, with good food trade. Long eating area and games bar with table football. Children allowed in games area. Food until 10 (not Mon). Swan necks but no sparklers. Small patio.

Pinkneys Green H1

A north-western suburb of Maidenhead, the village takes its name from Ghilo de Pinkney who owned it after the Norman invasion. The local swine pastures were mentioned in the Domesday Book; and in 1761 the area was known as Pigneys Green! It is now owned by the National Trust and offers wide-open spaces for a variety of leisure activities.

Golden Ball
Marlow Road (A308)
☎ (01628) 620938
11-11; 12-10.30 (Sun)
Boddington Bitter; Flower's Original; Morland Old Speckled Hen Ⓗ
Brewers Fayre house with large garden. Popular place to eat, especially in summer. Low beams on way to toilet are padded, but duck anyway!

Robin Hood
Marlow Road (A308)
☎ (01628) 626686
11.30-11; 12-10.30 (Sun)
Morland Original, Old Speckled Hen; Ruddles County Ⓗ
Very friendly roadside pub serving very good home-cooked meals. *Recommended.*
❀ ◐◑ ♿ ♣ P

Stag & Hounds
1 Lee Lane
☎ (01628) 630268
11-3, 5.30-11; 11-11 (Sat); 12-10.30 (Sun)
Arkell's 3B; Brakspear Bitter; Fuller's London Pride; Theakston Old Peculier; guest beers Ⓗ
Attractive little pub with its own skittle alley, set in rural surroundings. Large garden and extensive menu. Guest beers change frequently. *Recommended.*
❀ ◐◑ ♣ P

Waggon & Horses
112 Pinkneys Road
☎ (01628) 624429
11.30-3, 5-11; 11-4, 6-11 (Sat); 12-10.30 (Sun)
Morland Independent IPA; Ruddles Best, Draught Bass Ⓗ
Local with separate public bar. Darts and crib popular.

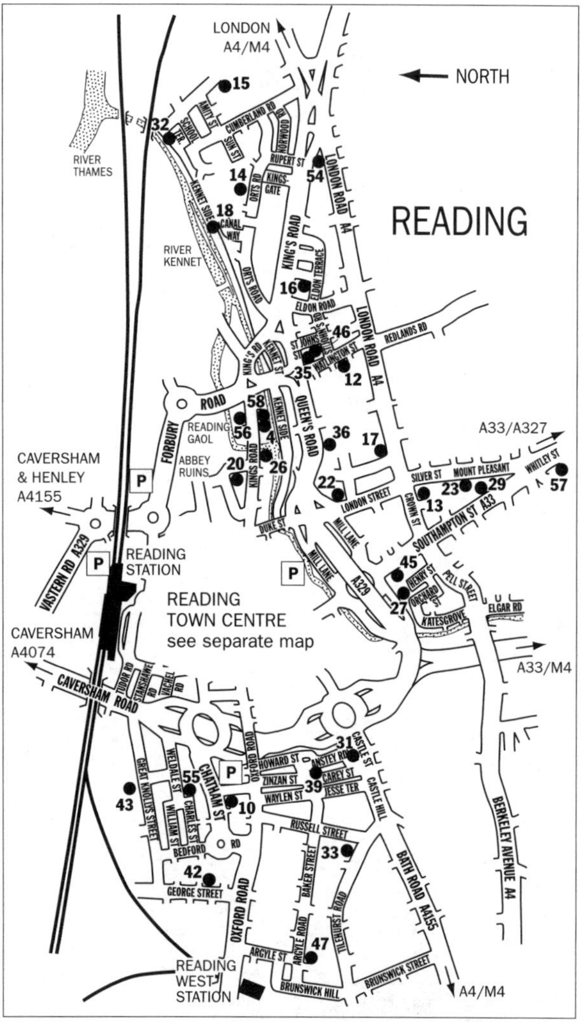

Reading F3

Although Berkshire no longer has an official county council, Reading is still considered to be the 'county town' (it is still seeking City status). Apart from being the largest conurbation in the shire, it is the main commercial, shopping and entertainment centre of the area. The town was, until fairly recently, renowned for its 'three Bs' – Beer, Bulbs and Biscuits. The beer came in the form of Simonds Brewery (although there were several others in the town) who eventually became part of the Courage empire and whose fine old Bridge Street Brewery has now been replaced by the Oracle shopping centre.

Keen gardeners will remember Suttons Seeds, who were the 'bulbs' part of the trio, with their head office and gardens where Suttons Business Park now stands. The company moved, a few years ago, to Devon.

As for the biscuits, this was probably the most famous name of all – Huntley & Palmers – whose impressive factory dominated the eastern end of the town, and whose

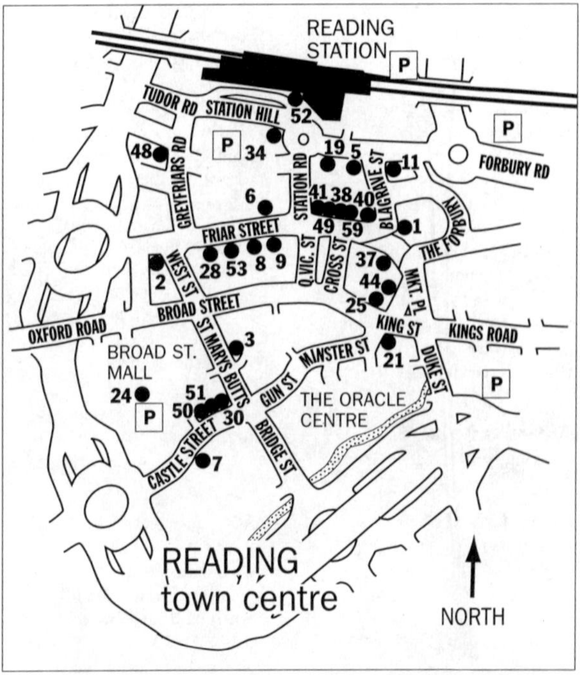

name still remains in the shape of parks and public amenities. There is a small section of the factory still standing, but the main site is now home to Prudential Insurance.

Just round the corner, across the canal, is Reading Gaol, made famous in a ballad by a certain inmate called Oscar Wilde. Next to the prison are the scanty remains of Reading Abbey where King Henry I was buried. The canal itself is actually the River Kennet and it joins the Thames just to the east of the town centre. Reading's university is home to the interesting Museum of English Rural Life and the town's terraced houses are noted for their distinctive local brickwork (note also the splendid architecture above the shop fronts in the town centre).

Courage still have a brewery (of sorts) in Reading but it only produces keg beers and lagers. Happily, however, there are three brew pubs in the town and the selection of real ales has grown over recent years, despite the proliferation of trendy theme bars and 'venues' which have opened up everywhere.

Reading is a major rail centre with services to all parts of the country including Gatwick airport and regular trains to London. There are plenty of bus services in the town and a coach link with Heathrow.

3 B's Bar, Old Town Hall ❶

Blagrave Street
☎ (0118) 939 9803
10-11; closed Sun
Beer range varies Ⓗ
Large bar which is part of Reading's old town hall. Live jazz Tue nights. Beer range often includes beers from Butts and West Berkshire Breweries. Named after Reading's three famous trades.

'Work is the curse of the drinking classes'

Oscar Wilde (1854–1900)

A Hooden in the Hat ❷
West Street
☎ (0118) 956 1735
11-11; 12-10.30 (Sun)
Greene King IPA, Abbot; guest beer Ⓗ
A small, town centre concept pub opened in June 1999. Wooden floor boards and basic chairs set the scene with music from the 50s and 60s played at a reasonable volume. A hooden is (apparently) a pantomime horse and the hat is a reference to the pub's former name, the Mitre. Beers served through swan neck and sparkler.

Alfred's Head
146 Chatham Street
No Real Ale.

Alley Cat Live
Gun Street
No Real Ale.

Allied Arms ❸
57 St Mary's Butts
☎ (0118) 959 0865
11-11; 12-6 (Sun)
Courage Best; Badger Tanglefoot Ⓗ
Local pub in town centre that, at one time, had its own brewery. Courtyard leads to garden.

Back of Beyond ❹
104–108 Kings Road (near A329)
☎ (0118) 959 5906
10-11; 12-10.30 (Sun)
Theakston Best; Fuller's London Pride; Courage Directors; Archers Golden; Hogs Back TEA; guest beers Ⓗ
Large Wetherspoon pub on the eastern side of town, built on the site of an old warehouse. Patio area at rear overlooking canal. *Recommended.*
Q ◐◑ ♿ ≠ ⚡

Battle Inn
2–4 Bedford Road
No Real Ale.

Ben's Bar & Thai Restaurant
Royal Court, King's Road
☎ (0118) 959 6169
11.30-3, 5-11; closed Sun
Fuller's London Pride Ⓗ
Canalside bar and restaurant on towpath opposite Prudential building.

Blagrave Arms ❺
35 Blagrave Street
☎ (0118) 959 0920
12-3, 6-11; closed Sun
Courage Best, Directors; Theakston Best Ⓗ
Time-warp pub full of wood and marble with a wonderful quiet atmosphere. A must to visit for its etched glasswork.

Boar's Head (Ye) ❻
26A Friar Street
☎ (0118) 958 0882
11-11; closed Sun
Webster's Green Label; Draught Bass; Greene King Abbot Ⓗ
Refurbished old town centre pub.

Brewery Tap ❼
27 Castle Street
☎ (0118) 957 6280
11-11; 12-10.30 (Sun)
Shepherd Neame Canterbury Jack, Spitfire; Tudor Brewery Red, Green; guest beers Ⓗ
Excellent conversion of former Courage social club to rustic ale house with on-site brewery using ex-pilot plant from Shepherd Neame. Food available all day. Large screen TV in rear 'brewery bar'; also available for functions. *Recommended.*
◐◑ ≠ ♣ ⚡

'The heart which grief
hath cankered,
Hath one unfailing
remedy – the Tankard'

Charles Stuart Calverley (1831–1884)

Broadwalk ❽
110–117 Friar Street
☎ (0118) 959 0692
11-11; 12-10.30 (Sun)
Fuller's Chiswick, London Pride, ESB Ⓗ
Brand new concept bar in town centre. Food and entertainment oriented. Large bar and seating area. Radio-controlled bouncers! *Recommended.*

Bugle ❾
144 Friar Street
☎ (0118) 957 3514
11-11; 12-4 (Sun)
Courage Best Ⓗ
Town centre locals' pub. Small public bar and larger lounge.

Butler ❿
89–91 Chatham Street
☎ (0118) 939 1635
11-11; 12-3, 7-10.30 (Sun)
Fuller's London Pride, ESB Ⓗ
Famous wine merchant premises, resident in Reading since Victorian times. One of Fuller's first ventures west from their west London homeland in 1970s. No food Sun eve. *Recommended.*

Carousel
Northumberland Avenue
No Real Ale.

Chronicles
17–19 Valpy Street
No Real Ale.

Claddagh Ring
Elgar Road
No Real Ale.

College Arms
128 Wokingham Road
No Real Ale.

Corn Exchange ⓫
Forbury Road
☎ (0118) 951 2340
12-11; closed Sun
Fuller's Chiswick, London Pride, ESB, seasonal beers Ⓗ
Former corn merchant's store, opened as a pub in 1994 after rebuilding. Worth visiting to see the architecture and machinery. *Recommended.*

County Arms ⓬
84 Watlington Street
☎ (0118) 959 0666
11-3, 5-11; 12-3, 6-10.30 (Sun)
Morland Original, IPA, Old Speckled Hen Ⓗ
Very clean and tidy, spacious one-bar town pub. Beer patio outside.

Crown ⓭
23 Crown Street
☎ (0118) 975 2768
11-11; 12-10.30 (Sun)
Guest beer Ⓗ
Basic two-bar local. Landlord is a real ale fan with a vast collection of pump clips. *Recommended.*

Dove ⓮
119 Orts Road
☎ (0118) 935 2556
12-2.30, 6-11; 12-3, 6-11 (Sat); 12-4, 7-10.30 (Sun)
Brakspear Bitter, Special Ⓗ
Wonderful two-bar friendly community local with handsome exterior. Occasional live music. Pool table and darts. No food Sat or Sun. *Recommended.*

Eastgate ⓯
59 Cholmeley Road
☎ (0118) 926 2844
5-11; 11-11 (Sat); 12-10.30 (Sun)
Courage Best Ⓗ
Two-bar locals' pub with large garden. The name refers to the east gate of Reading Abbey.

Edwards
12 Station Road
No Real Ale.

Eldon Arms ⓰
19 Eldon Terrace (off Eldon Road)
☎ (0118) 957 3857
10.30-3, 5.30-11; 12-3, 7-10.30 (Sun)
Wadworth IPA, 6X, Old Timer, seasonal beers; guest beers Ⓗ
Lively backstreet pub with live music evenings. Large public bar, smaller lounge.
Recommended.
Q ⊞ ≠

Engineer's Arms
Whitley Wood Lane
Closed.

Fez & Firkin ⓱
31 London Road
☎ (0118) 957 6930
11.30-11; 12-10.30 (Sun)
Firkin Fez, Best, Dogbolter; guest beer Ⓗ
Part coaching inn, part modern extension. Music- and student-oriented: near university halls of residence.

Fisherman's Cottage ⓲
224 Kennetside (off Orts Road)
☎ (0118) 957 1553
11-11; 12-10.30 (Sun)
Fuller's Chiswick, London Pride, ESB, seasonal beers Ⓗ
Very popular canalside pub extended and conservatory added. Hidden away from road; easier to find on foot.
Recommended.
♛ Q ♘ ◐ ♿ ♣ P

Flyer & Firkin ⓳
53 Blagrave Street
☎ (0118) 956 9151
11-11; 12-10.30 (Sun)
Firkin Best, Flyer, Dogbolter Ⓗ
Large, boisterous, typical Firkin pub opposite Reading station with own brewery viewed through small conservatory. Three pool tables. Small patio at rear. TV screens scattered throughout. Food 12–8.30. DJ Saturdays. *Recommended.*
❀ ◐ ≠

Forbury Vaults ⓴
21 Abbey Square
☎ (0118) 957 4461
11-11; closed Sun
Modern town pub hidden away down a side street (off King's Road). *For sale at time of survey.*

Foresters Arms
Brunswick Street
No Real Ale.

Four Horseshoes
177 Basingstoke Road
☎ (0118) 987 1604
Fuller's London Pride Ⓗ
Vast brick edifice on the Basingstoke road. Large wood-panelled Edwardian bar (public bar). Lounge bar closed at time of survey.

Froggies
Queens Walk
No Real Ale.

George & Dragon
162 Bath Road
☎ (0118) 959 0694
11-11; 12-10.30 (Sun)
Morland Original, Independent IPA; guest beer Ⓗ
Large roadside pub with one bar and children's area. Guest beer changes regularly.
Recommended.
♘ ❀ ◐ P

George Hotel (Cock 'n' Bull Bar) ㉑
10–12 King Street
☎ (0118) 957 3445/958 1688
11-11; 12-10.30 (Sun)
Courage Directors Ⓗ
Newly refurbished former coaching inn with cobbled courtyard. Real ale not always available.

Granby Tavern
120 London Road
No Real Ale.

Great Expectations ㉒
33 London Street
☎ (0118) 950 3925
11-11; 12-3, 7-10.30 (Sun)
Courage Best; Fuller's London Pride; Gales HSB Ⓗ
Large town bar with Dickensian theme and tableaux. Pool table,

bouncers and late licence till 2 am Fri and Sat. Beer range varies.

Greyhound ㉓
4 Mount Pleasant
☎ (0118) 975 6335
11–11; 12–10.30 (Sun)
Badger Tanglefoot; guest beers Ⓗ
Two-bar town pub. Future uncertain under its current owners (Inntrepreneur).

Ha! Ha!
Kings Road
No Real Ale.

Happy Prospect
Coronation Square
No Real Ale.

Harvester
Underwood Shopping Precinct, Holymead, Fords Farm
No Real Ale.

Harvey Floorbanger's
61 St Mary Butts
No Real Ale.

Hexagon Theatre ㉔
Queens Walk
☎ (0118) 939 0016
11.30–3 (other opening varies)
Theakston XB; Marston's Pedigree Ⓗ
Theatre bar and café opens one hour before show begins. Outside patio/garden.

Hobgoblin ㉕
2 Broad Street
☎ (0118) 950 8119
11–11; 12–10.30 (Sun)
Beer range varies Ⓗ
An excellent beer drinkers' pub with no frills but a friendly welcome and good beer. Usually three beers from the Wychwood range plus five ever-changing guests, mainly from small independent breweries. Provides a very welcome change from the theme pubs which dominate this area of town. *Recommended.*
⇌

Hobgoblin
344A Oxford Road
☎ (0118) 957 3126
12–11; 12–10.30 (Sun)
Wychwood Special Ⓗ
Lively pub next to Battle hospital. Popular with the Irish community. Near Reading West station.

Hogshead ㉖
76–78 Kings Road
☎ (0118) 958 6549
11–11; 12–10.30 (Sun)
Beer range varies Ⓗ/Ⓖ
Typical conversion by Whitbread of former shop premises – now a spacious alehouse on two floors with flagstones and wooden beams. Outside patios on both floors. Small range of Belgian beers, some of which are bottle-conditioned. A hogshead is a large beer cask containing 54 gallons. *Recommended.*
Q ♿ 🚭

Hook & Tackle ㉗
Katesgrove Lane (near flyover)
☎ (0118) 950 0830
11–11; 12–10.30 (Sun)
Courage Directors; Fuller's London Pride, ESB; Greene King IPA Ⓗ
Fine backstreet local: Reading's first freehouse. Beer quality can vary.

Hope Tap ㉘
99–101 Friar Street
☎ (0118) 958 2266
10–11; 12–10.30 (Sun)
Beer range varies Ⓗ
Large pub decorated in typical Wetherspoon style. Patio area at back. The name derives from the short-lived Hope Brewery which was established on the site c. 1830. *Recommended.*
❀ ◐ ♿ ⇌ 🚭

'I will make it a felony to drink small beer'

William Shakespeare (1564–1616)

Hop Leaf ㉙

163–165 Southampton Street (A33)
☎ (0118) 931 4700
4-11 (Mon, Tue); 12-2, 4-11 (Wed-Fri); 12-11 (Sat); 12-10.30 (Sun)
Hop Back GFB, Best, Stout, Summer Lightning; guest beers Ⓗ
Top-notch basic but friendly boozer with an excellent range of beers, including beers from Reading Lion brewery at back of premises. Small meeting room available. Bar billiards. Local CAMRA branch pub of the year 1999. *Recommended.*
♣

Horn ㉚

2 Castle Street
☎ (0118) 957 4794
11-11; 12-10.30 (Sun)
Courage Best; Theakston XB Ⓗ
Listed 16th-century, timbered town centre local. The name refers to the post-horn used by stage coach guards. *Recommended.*
❀◐

Horncastle

208 Bath Road (A4)
☎ (0118) 945 1265
11-11; 12-10.30 (Sun)
Smiles Best; Charles Wells Bombardier Ⓗ
Basic, friendly, no-frills local named after sub-district to west of town. Small, well-lived-in saloon, large public bar and games room which is also available for private functions. Some original features including three fireplaces. Small garden at rear.

Horse & Jockey ㉛

120 Castle Street (off A329)
☎ (0118) 959 0172
11-11; 12-10.30 (Sun)
Archers Village; guest beers Ⓗ
Good, friendly local, situated next to inner ring road near Salvation Army, with enthusiastic landlord. Prior to takeover by Greene King, twice voted pub of the year by local CAMRA branch. Still owned by Greene King but no longer sells their beers. *Recommended.*
♔◐♣

Jolly Anglers ㉜

Kennet Side
☎ (0118) 926 1666
11-11; 12-10.30 (Sun)
Theakston XB; Fuller's London Pride Ⓗ
Canalside, two-bar pub with a country pub atmosphere. Outside tables in summer. *Recommended.*
♿♣

Jolly Brewers ㉝

12 Tilehurst Road
☎ (0118) 958 1745
11-11; 12-10.30 (Sun)
Greene King Abbot; Draught Bass Ⓗ
Modern one-bar pub with pool table and restaurant area.

Jolly Porter ㉞

37 Station Road
☎ (0118) 958 2493
12-11; 12-6 (Sun)
Courage Best Ⓗ
Modern basic bar opposite Reading station. Occasionally closes for private functions.

J.W.'s

1 Gun Street
No Real Ale.

King's Tavern

252 Kings Road
No Real Ale.

Lion

21 Great Knollys Street
No Real Ale.

Lyndhurst Alehouse ㉟

88 Queen's Road
☎ (0118) 957 4615
11-11; 12-10.30 (Sun)
Boddingtons Bitter; Whitbread Trophy; Wadworth 6X, Gales HSB Ⓗ
Despite the name, the range has been greatly reduced following opening of nearby Hogshead; none on stillage. Very much a young person's pub. Can be noisy.

MacDevitts ㊱
21 South Street
☎ (0118) 901 5236
12-3, 6-11; 12-3 (Mon); closed Sun
Wadworth 6X Ⓗ
Part of the South Street Arts Centre. Live music evenings and pub food.

Maidens
234 Shinfield Road
☎ (0118) 987 1481
11-11; 12-10.30 (Sun)
Webster's Green Label, **Greene King** Abbot Ⓗ
Formerly called the Merry Maidens, this is probably Reading's largest pub. Large Sky Sports screen in games area which has bar billiards and pool. Food served including Sun lunch. It could almost be described as a licensed art gallery and there are some interesting items of breweriana.

Malthouse
53 Greyfriars Road
No Real Ale.

Mansion House
Prospect Park
No Real Ale.

Moderation
231 Caversham Road
☎ (0118) 957 4172
11-11; 12-10.30 (Sun)
Fuller's London Pride Ⓗ
Street corner local with pool tables, etc. Beer served through swan neck and sparkler. B&B available.

Monk's Retreat ㊲
163 Friar Street
☎ (0118) 950 7592
10-11; 12-10.30 (Sun)
Beer range varies Ⓗ
Deceptively large town centre pub. Wetherspoon's first outlet in Reading, recently repainted inside and out. *Recommended.*
◐◑♿⇌⚡

Nag's Head
5 Russell Street
No Real Ale.

Newt & Cucumber ㊳
12–14 Friar Street
☎ (0118) 958 1457
11-11; closed Sun
Ruddles Best; **Morland** Old Speckled Hen Ⓗ
Themed town centre bar/restaurant with large wooden floor area. Due to be sold to Mansfield Brewery.

Northumberland Arms
75 Northumberland Avenue
☎ (0118) 987 1861
11-11; 12-10.30 (Sun)
Usher's Best; Seasonal beers Ⓗ
Smart, modern two-bar suburban pub.

Oasis ㊴
19–21 Baker Street
☎ (0118) 957 6978
11.30-11; 12-10.30 (Sun)
Morland Original; **Ruddles** Best Ⓗ
Backstreet pub just west of town centre. Emphasis on pool. Lunch and evening meals.

Old Society ㊵
5–6 Friar Street
☎ (0118) 959 0614
11-11; 12-10.30 (Sun)
Greene King IPA, Abbot Ⓗ
Pleasantly converted modern bar, in premises previously belonging to a building society, hence the name. Greene King's first Reading outlet. *Recommended.*
❀◐◑♿⇌⚡

Pavlov's Dog
St Mary Butts
No Real Ale.

Plasterer's Arms
38–40 Rupert Walk
No Real Ale.

Pheasant
225 Southampton Street
No Real Ale.

Pitcher & Piano (41)
Friar Street
☎ (0118) 958 8964
11-11; 12-10.30 (Sun)
Marston's Pedigree Ⓗ
Large, smart café style bar; the latest of numerous young people's venues within a very short space along Friar Street. Food available at most times.

Pond House
738 Oxford Road (A329)
☎ (0118) 957 2119
11-11; 12-10.30 (Sun)
Whitbread Trophy Ⓗ
Spacious town pub with three pool tables, 'bowlarama' bowling alley, Sky TV, etc. Open until late Fri and Sat nights.

Purple Turtle
9 Gun Street
☎ (0118) 959 7196
No draught Real Ale but some bottle-conditioned beers.

Queen Elizabeth (42)
21 George Street
☎ (0118) 957 6630
5-11; 12-11 (Sat); 12-3, 7-10.30 (Sun)
Fuller's London Pride; **Wadworth** 6X Ⓗ
Pleasant backstreet local, close to central swimming pool and Reading West station.

Queen's Arms (43)
24 Great Knollys Street
☎ (0118) 959 0143
11-3, 6-11; 12-4, 7-10.30 (Sun)
Morland Original, Old Speckled Hen; guest beer Ⓗ
Recently refurbished one-bar pub next to bus depot. Meals 12–2, 6.30–9 (not Sun eve).

Queen's Head
54 Christchurch Road
☎ (0118) 986 1279
11.30-11; 12-10.30 (Sun)
Theakston XB; **Courage** Best; **John Smith's** Bitter; guest beer Ⓗ
Two-bar busy local. Closest pub to university; student-oriented during term-time. *Recommended.*
❀◑⊞♣

Rat & Parrot (44)
29–31 Market Place
☎ (0118) 957 2238
11-11; 12-10.30 (Sun)
Courage Directors; **Theakston** Best; **Brakspear** Special Ⓗ
Large and unusual town-centre theme pub with differently styled drinking areas.

Red Cow
50 Crown Street
No Real Ale.

Red Lion (45)
34 Southampton Street
☎ (0118) 957 3243
11-11; 12-10.30 (Sun)
Fuller's London Pride Ⓗ
Large three-roomed pub. 'No travellers.' Beer served through tight sparkler.

Retreat (46)
8 St Johns Street (off A329)
☎ (0118) 957 1593
11-11; 12-10.30 (Sun)
Flowers IPA; **Wadworth** 6X; guest beers Ⓗ
A gem of a pub hidden in small backstreet which appears to have been unchanged during the last century. Small snug bar and larger bar at rear with pool and darts. A pub for all age groups. Occasional folk music (Thur eve). Parking difficult. *Recommended.*
⊞♣

Rising Sun (Tut 'n' Shive)
Forbury Road
No Real Ale.

Rose & Thistle (47)
Argyle Road (near A329)
☎ NOT LISTED
11-11; 12-10.30 (Sun)
Courage Best; **Greene King** IPA, Abbot Ⓗ
Comfortable backstreet local with a pleasant garden. The name refers to the linking of England with Scotland. Close to Reading West station. Meals served 12–10 every day. *Recommended.*
❀◑⇌♣

Roundhead
Coley Park
No Real Ale.

Royal Albion
642 Oxford Road (A329)
☎ (0118) 957 4583
12–11; 11–11 (Fri, Sat); 12–10.30 (Sun)
Morland Original, Independent IPA Ⓗ
Large lounge bar with prominent wide-screen TV and smaller public bar with pool table. Very busy at weekends. Albion is a poetic name for Britain.

Scruffy Murphy's (48)
31–33 Greyfriars Road
☎ (0118) 959 0376
12–11; 12–10.30 (Sun)
Tetley Bitter Ⓗ
Irish theme pub. Live music every Thur and Sat. Formerly the Railway Tavern.

Southcote
Southcote Lane (off A4)
☎ (0118) 957 2685
12–11; 12–10.30 (Sun)
Boddingtons Bitter; Wadworth 6X; Marston's Pedigree Ⓗ
Attractive and comfortable roadside Beefeater pub/restaurant, with standard formula decor and menu. Family friendly with baby-changing facilities. Restaurant closed 2.30–6.30. Large car park and garden. Named after Reading sub-district.

Sportsman
201 Shinfield Road
☎ (0118) 987 5713
11–11; 12–3, 7–10.30 (Sun)
Morland Original; Ruddles Best Ⓗ
Two-bar pub with noisy games bar and a comfortable lounge. Lives up to its name with sporting activities most nights and live music Saturdays. Attractive Art Nouveau fireplace in the lounge.

Spread Eagle
117 Norfolk Road
☎ (0118) 957 3558
11.45–3, 5.30–11; 12–11 (Sat); 12–10.30 (Sun)
Morland Original, Tanner's Jack, Independent IPA Ⓗ
Multi-roomed pub with large lounge/restaurant, games and family rooms. Opposite extinct Elm Park football ground but retains many associations with the club. Real gem of a family local. *Recommended.*
Q ◐◑ ♣ P

Square (The) (49)
Friar Street
☎ (0118) 958 9136
12–11; 12–10.30 (Sun)
Wadworth 6X Ⓗ
Fantastic cocktail lounge bar in town centre. Has to be seen and be seen in. Revolving video cube in its sunken middle.

Sun (50)
16 Castle Street
☎ (0118) 957 5106
11–11; 12–10.30 (Sun)
Courage Best; Theakston Best; Wadworth 6X; Brakspear Special Ⓗ
Ancient (16th-century) town pub with several drinking areas and strong bar billiards following. *Recommended.*
❀ ◐◑ P

Sweeney & Todd (51)
10 Castle Street
☎ (0118) 958 6466
11–10.30; closed Sun
Adnams Bitter; Wadworth 6X; Thomas Hardy Royal Oak; guest beers Ⓗ
A most unlikely looking pub which is actually an ale and pie shop situated in a conservation area of town. Traditional English food to supplement the beer. Open for breakfast. *Recommended.*
Q ◐◑ ≉

see page 126

Three Men in a Boat
Richfield Avenue
☎ (0118) 925 9988
12-11; 12-10.30 (Sun)
Flowers Original; Fuller's London Pride; Wadworth 6X Ⓗ
Large riverside establishment, part of the Holiday Inn complex. Outside area in summer on the river bank. *Recommended.*
🛏 ◐ ◑ ♿ P

Three Guineas 52
Station Approach
☎ (0118) 957 2743
10-11; 12-10.30 (Sun)
Great Western Bitter; Brakspear Bitter; Young's Bitter; Gales HSB; Draught Bass Ⓗ
Large active pub on Reading station (front entrance or platform 4) often frequented by commuters. Open early for food: breakfast served all day. Full menu 10–3, basket food 3–8. Great Western Bitter is Hancock's. Seating outside on pedestrianised area. Named after prize awarded by GWR in competition for naming record-breaking train.

Three Tuns
191 Wokingham Road
☎ (0118) 926 2170
11-11; 12-10.30 (Sun)
Courage Best, Directors; Greene King Abbot Ⓗ
Large detached pub with two bars and many TVs. Three pool tables. Large patio with aviary.

Tudor Tavern 53
Friar Street
☎ (0118) 957 3176
11-11; 12-6 (Sun)
Draught Bass Ⓗ
Long shoe-box bar with mock Tudor woodwork. Great potential for future development.

'A woman drove me to drink and I never had the courtesy to thank her'

W.C. Fields

Upin Arms 54
151 London Road
☎ NOT LISTED
11-11; 12-10.30 (Sun)
Draught Bass Ⓗ
Part of the Bass 'It's a Scream' chain, this noisy young person's pub is not for the sensitive-natured. Previously called the Jack of Both Sides, the name has now been changed to a hilarious pun.

Wallingford Arms 55
2 Caroline Street
☎ (0118) 957 5272
11-11; 12-10.30 (Sun)
Morland Original; Draught Bass Ⓗ
Typical backstreet local, close to the town centre. Beer quality varies.

Warwick Arms 56
77 Kings Road
☎ (0118) 950 0412
11-11; 11-6 (Sat); 12-6 (Sun)
Morland Original; guest beers Ⓗ
A large, lively and loud Morland 'free house' with a changing range of beers.

Wellington Arms 57
72 Whitley Street
☎ (0118) 987 1542
11-11; 12-10.30 (Sun)
Courage Best; guest beer Ⓗ
Recently acquired by Enterprise Inns pub group and real ale reintroduced following refurbishment. Small garden area at the back.

Whitley Tavern
40 Northumberland Avenue
☎ (0118) 954 7753
11-11; 12-10.30 (Sun)
Courage Best; Fuller's London Pride; Webster's Green Label Ⓗ
Modern estate pub with spacious lounge and patio area. Beer range may vary.

Woodley Arms
Waldeck Street
No Real Ale.

Wishing Well
280 Oxford Road (A329)
☎ (0118) 959 7991
11–11; 12–10.30 (Sun)
Ushers Best Ⓗ
Small Irish bar opened in December 1998 in former pizza shop. TVs in almost every corner. Beer may change.

World Turned Upside Down
387 Basingstoke Road (A33)
☎ (0118) 987 1763
11–11; 12–10.30 (Sun)
Fuller's London Pride Ⓗ
Themed Harvester Restaurant with Forte Travelodge attached. Outside play area.

Wynford Arms (58)
110 Kings Road
☎ (0118) 958 9814
12–11; 12–10.30 (Sun)
Wadworth 6X, Courage Best Ⓗ
Tidy town pub. Reading's premier gay pub.

Yates's Wine Lodge (59)
7 Friar Street
☎ (0118) 959 7090
11–11; 12–10.30 (Sun)
Boddingtons Bitter Ⓗ
Reading's converted main post office, now a vast two-storey, galleried drinking emporium with bouncers on the door. Disabled access and no-smoking area. Beer served through swan neck and sparkler.

Remenham F1

Just over the bridge from Henley-on-Thames.

Little Angel
Remenham Lane (near A423)
☎ (01491) 574165
12–3, 5–11; 12–3, 6–10.30 (Sun)
Brakspear Bitter, Special, seasonal beers Ⓗ
Up-market 18th-century inn of historic and architectural interest near Henley bridge. Heavy emphasis on food with separate restaurant but the beer is rather expensive.

Two Brewers
Wargrave Road (A321)
☎ (01491) 574375
12–2.30, 5–11; 12–2.30, 7–11 (Sun)
Brakspear Bitter, seasonal beers Ⓗ
Cosy pub, tucked away down from busy road junction close to Henley bridge. Often quiet during the day but gets busier at weekends. The 'brewers' refers to the draymen who delivered the beer by foot from nearby Henley, by means of a cask slung from a pole.

Riseley F4

Nearby are Wellington Country Park and Stratfield Saye House – the 17th-century home of the Duke of Wellington.

Bull
Basingstoke Road (B3349)
☎ (0118) 988 3194
11.30–3, 6–11; 12–3, 7–10.30 (Sun)
Shepherd Neame Best Bitter, Master Brew, Spitfire Ⓗ
One-bar roadside establishment.

Dog & Partridge
Basingstoke Road (B3349)
☎ (0118) 988 3406
12–2.30, 6–11; 12–3, 7–10.30 (Sun)
Flowers Original; Fuller's London Pride Ⓗ
Tidy village local with two bars and large skittle alley.

Ruscombe G2

Royal Oak
Ruscombe Lane (B3024)
☎ (0118) 934 5190
10.30–2.30; 7–11 (Sat); 12–3, 7–10.30 (Sun)
Wadworth 6X; Brakspear Bitter; Webster's Green Label Ⓗ
Comfortable, roomy pub aimed at no particular type of clientele. Pleasant garden patio area. Rather lacking in atmosphere of any kind. Emphasis on food.

Salt Hill J2

A western suburb of Slough, named after the ancient Montem Ceremony whereby travellers had to pay a toll in salt before continuing along the Bath Road.

Three Tuns
124 Bath Road (A4)
☎ (01753) 521911
11–11; 12–10.30 (Sun)
Courage Best, Directors; Brakspear Special Ⓗ
Comfortable roadside house in district just west of main shopping area. Refurbished November 1998 and trying hard to become a community local.

Windmill
104 Bath Road (A4)
☎ (01753) 526964
11–11; 12–10.30 (Sun)
Flowers Original; Wadworth 6X; Marston's Pedigree Ⓗ
A standard 'Crowded House' branded pub with in-house restaurant.

Sandhurst G4

An urban development which borders on Hampshire and Surrey and is famous for its Royal Military Academy and National Army Museum. It is now a mecca for shoppers to The Meadows complex.

Bull & Butcher
234 Yorktown Road, College Town (A321)
☎ (01276) 32489
12–2.30, 5–11; 12–11 (Fri, Sat); 12–10.30 (Sun)
Courage Best; Fuller's London Pride Ⓗ
Friendly pub popular with locals. Mostly unspoilt building retains some original features including art deco glasswork. Large and varied food menu (not Sunday evening). Originally, the pub name was a reference to the beheading of Anne Boleyn.

Duke's Head
High Street (A321)
☎ (01252) 873083
12–3, 5.30–11; 12–3, 5.30–10.30 (Sun)
Morland Original Ⓗ
Single open-plan bar with pleasant local atmosphere. Live music Thur. Piano and toilet in bar!

Jolly Farmer
Yorktown Road (A321)
College Town
☎ (01276) 33590
11–11; 12–10.30 (Sun)
Courage Best, Directors Ⓗ
Basic but friendly pub with a small conservatory area built on to the lounge bar where children are welcome, in addition to mini adventure playground in garden. Close to Royal Military Academy and superstores at The Meadows.

New Inn
Crowthorne Road (off A321)
☎ (01252) 873220
11–11; 12–10.30 (Sun)
Fuller's London Pride; occasional guest beer Ⓗ
Down-to-earth street corner pub with a sporting theme. Fuller's beer has a strong following with the locals. Cheap beer Thur eve.

Rackstraw Farm
221 Yorktown Road (A321)
☎ (01252) 878181
11–11; 12–10.30 (Sun)
Boddingtons Bitter; Wadworth 6X; Marston's Pedigree Ⓗ
Pub housed in a converted

farmhouse, named after Jack Rackstraw, an 18th-century farm owner. Standard Beefeater decor but the fact that the restaurant is in a totally separate building gives the pub more of a genuine feel. Popular with young people. Travel Lodge next door.

Rose & Crown
108 High Street
☎ (01252) 872332
11-3, 5-11; 11-11 (Thur-Sat); 12-10.30 (Sun)
Ushers Best, Founders Ⓗ
Emphatically a young person's pub with very loud music. Large, pleasant garden and games room. Can be very smoky. Karaoke features. Food available 12–2.30, 5.30–8; 12–8 (9 summer) Sat, Sun.

Wellington Arms
Yorktown Road (A321)
☎ (01252) 872408
11-11; 12-10.30 (Sun)
Brakspear Bitter, Special Ⓗ
Basic 18th-century pub whose main bar can be lively. The comfortable lounge, which was added in the late 20th century, can usually provide a more relaxed atmosphere for a quiet drink. Food available at most times: 'Steak night' every Friday from 6–9. Skittle alley (up to 40 people). *Recommended.*
❀ ◐◑ ♣ P

White Swan
Swan Lane (off A321)
☎ (01252) 872444
11-11; 12-10.30 (Sun)
Morland Independent IPA, Original, Old Speckled Hen; Ruddles Best Ⓗ
Lively sidestreet pub backing on to the Yateley Lakes. TV screens, fruit machines and loud music add to the boisterous atmosphere. The pool table is very popular.

Shaw C3

Cock Inn
108 Shaw Road (B4009)
No Real Ale.

Robin Hood
London Road (A4)
No Real Ale.

Shefford Woodlands A3

Pheasant
Baydon Road
☎ (01484) 648284
11-3, 5.15-11; 11-11 (Fri); 12-3, 7-10.30 (Sun)
Brakspear Bitter; Wadworth 6X; Ruddles County; Butts Bitter, Barbus Barbus Ⓗ
Fine old building whose public bar has fittings which date from before WW2. Small comfortable lounge and high standard restaurant. Although only a quarter of a mile from M4 junction 13, it has a genuine rural feel. Very popular with rugby coaches. Pub games include 'Ring the Bull'. *Recommended.*
🜂 Q ❀ ◐◑ ⊟ ♣ P

Shinfield F3

Bell & Bottle
School Green (B3349)
☎ (0118) 988 3563
11.30-11; 12-10.30 (Sun)
Rebellion Mild; Archers Village; Courage Best; Wadworth 6X; guest beers Ⓗ
Popular two-bar freehouse with garden and patio area. Up to four other beers available. Beer sparklers will be removed on request. Planning permission gained April 1999 to extend, incorporating adjacent barn into main structure with the addition of disabled toilets. *Recommended.*
🜂 ❀ ◐◑ ⊟ ♿ ♣ P

Black Boy
Shinfield Road (A327)
☎ (0118) 988 3116
11-11; 12-10.30 (Sun)
Morland Original, Old Speckled Hen; **Ruddles** County Ⓗ
One-bar roadside pub with restaurant. Small garden area in car park.

Royal Oak
39 School Green (B3349)
☎ (0118) 988 2931
11-11; 12-10.30 (Sun)
Morland Original, Old Speckled Hen; **Ruddles** Best Ⓗ
Friendly village local with two bars and attached marquee. Small garden. Good food. *Recommended.*
❀ ◐◑ ♿ ♣ P

Six Bells (Hungry Horse)
Church Lane
☎ (0118) 988 3526
11-11; 12-10.30 (Sun)
Greene King IPA, Abbot; Draught **Bass** Ⓗ
Themed restaurant pub in rural setting away from Shinfield village but close to M4 motorway.

Shurlock Row G3

Royal Oak
Hungerford Lane
☎ (0118) 934 5133
Opening varies
Morland Original, Old Speckled Hen; **Adnams** Broadside Ⓗ
Although this establishment still looks like a pub from outside, it is, in fact, a restaurant with little provision for drinkers who do not wish to dine.

'Man, being responsible, must get drunk; The best of life is but intoxication'

Lord Byron (1788–1824)

White Hart
(off) Straight Mile (B3018)
☎ (0118) 934 3301
12-2.30, 7-11; 12-3, 7-10.30 (Sun)
Brakspear Bitter; **Fuller's** London Pride ; **Wadworth** 6X Ⓗ
Smart and comfortable pub with huge fireplace dividing the main drinking area offering a very warm welcome in winter. The walls are splendidly decorated with brasses and other paraphernalia collected by the long-standing landlord. A few remnants of Wethered's brewery give a clue to the pub's history. No food Sun eve. *Recommended.*
❀ ◐◑ P

Sindlesham F3

Poacher
Mill Lane (near B3270)
☎ NOT LISTED
11-2.30, 5.30-11; 11-11 (Sat); 12-10.30 (Sun)
Marston's Pedigree; **Fuller's** London Pride; **Wadworth** 6X Ⓗ
Large converted mill building, with wooden floorboards, on the Loddon; accessed via narrow bridges. Part of Queen's Moat hotel. Aimed mainly at younger clientele, with noisy music and TVs. Large patio area gets busy in Summer.

Walter Arms
Bearwood Road (near B3030)
☎ (0118) 978 0260
11-3, 5-11; 12 -3, 6-10.30 (Sun)
Marston's Pedigree; **Courage** Best; **Young's** Special Ⓗ
Splendid Victorian structure houses upmarket pub with emphasis on food. Wooden pews made comfortable with an abundance of cushions. Business lunch menu faxed on request. May be closed Sunday evenings.

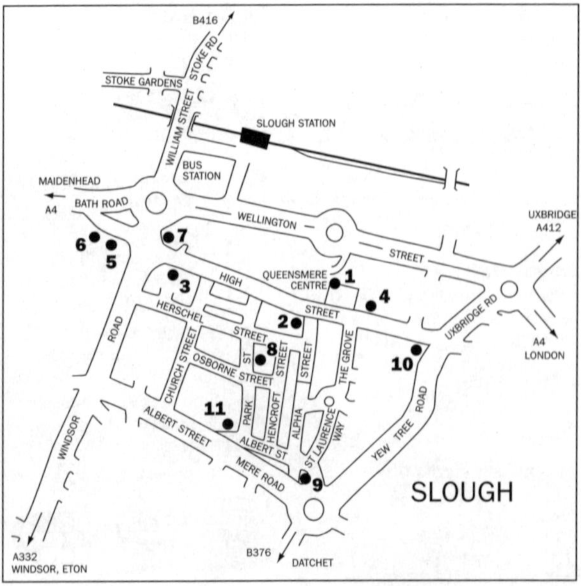

Slough J2

John Betjeman's bombs never did fall on Slough, so this large industrial town survives (under the shadow of Windsor Castle and the Heathrow flightpath).

A number of new town centre mega-pubs have sprung up in recent years but there are still a few backstreet boozers left and some decent pubs in the suburbs. The town is well served by both bus and rail services with fast trains to Reading and London.

Alpha Arms
Alpha Street North
No Real Ale.

Broadwalk ❶
Queensmere Shopping Centre (access from High Street)
☎ (01753) 532342
10-11; 10-12 (Thu-Sat); 12-10.30 (Sun)
Fuller's Chiswick, London Pride, ESB Ⓗ
Large, split-level hostelry with island bar and covered patio area. Full menu until 7. Happy hour 5–7 Mon–Fri. Opens at 10 for breakfast (no alcohol served till 11). Disabled access and toilets.

Cherry Picker
Stoke Poges Lane
No Real Ale.

Coachmakers Arms
Church Street
No Real Ale.

Dolphin
Uxbridge Road
No Real Ale.

Floral Arms ❷
228 High Street
☎ (01753) 523417
11-11; 12-4 (Sun)
Courage Best; Greene King Abbot Ⓗ
One-bar locals' pub at end of pedestrian area. Name recently changed back to its original from Pickled Newt and the signs will be changed as part of upcoming refurbishment. Everyone in Slough called it the Floral, anyway! Beer range likely to change after makeover. Food available 12.30–2.30 and 5.30–7.30 Mon–Sat. *Recommended.*
❀ ◑ ≥ ♣

Golden Cross
Wexham Road
No Real Ale.

Good Companions
93 Stoke Poges Lane
No Real Ale.

Goose in the Town ❸
106–110 High Street (near A4)
☎ (01753) 786011
11–11; 12–10.30 (Sun)
Goose Ale; Draught **Bass**; **Fuller's** London Pride; guest beer Ⓗ
Large, new single-bar pub opened in 1998. Food available all day. *Recommended.*
Q ◐ ◗ ♿ ⇌ ⚡

Greyhound
116 Albert Street
No Real Ale.

Herschel Arms
22 Park Street
No Real Ale.

Jolly Londoner
Wentworth Avenue, Britwell
No Real Ale.

Lighthouse
272A High Street
No Real Ale.

Litten Tree ❹
281 High Street
12–12; 12–11 (Sun)
Courage Best, Directors; **Litten Tree** Best Ⓗ
Originally intended to be a nightclub, hence the disco dance floor in the upstairs bar. No-smoking area.

Lynch Pin
Long Furlong Drive, Britwell
No Real Ale.

Moon & Spoon ❺
86 High Street
☎ (01753) 531650
11–11; 12–10.30 (Sun)
Courage Directors; **Fuller's** London Pride; **Theakston** Best; guest beers Ⓗ
Large, split-level Wetherspoon's pub with mixed clientele, reflecting cosmopolitan nature of

the district. Popular with business people at lunchtimes and younger customers Fri and Sat eve. Cheapest beer in Slough. Food available until one hour before closing. *Recommended.*

Nag's Head
167 Elliman Avenue
☎ (01753) 551964
11-11; 12-10.30 (Sun)
Courage Best; John Smith's Bitter Ⓗ
Lovely two-bar community pub. Popular both with locals and boating people from the nearby Grand Union canal. Food 12–2 Mon–Fri. *Recommended.*
P

Newt & Cucumber ❻
80 High Street
☎ (01753) 511818
11.30-11; opening varies-10.30 (Sun)
Flowers Original, Morland Old Speckled Hen; Ruddles Best Ⓗ
Large, modern and youth oriented. Food available throughout the day. Happy hours 12–2 Mon–Thur and 5–7 Mon–Fri. Sunday opening depends on televised sport.

O'Neil's
20 Windsor Road
No Real Ale.

Phrenologist & Firkin ❼
93–95 William Street
☎ (01753) 532439
11-11; 12-10.30 (Sun)
Firkin Best Bitter, Phrenologist Ale, Dogbolter Ⓗ
Huge warehouse of a pub, converted from insurance company office. Typically brash Firkin outlet. Frequent live entertainment. Beers come from Birmingham. Patio at front. Food available until 8.30. No-smoking area.

Pied Horse
300 High Street
No Real Ale.

Pitcher's Sports Bar
92 High Street
No Real Ale.

Printers Devil
19 Stoke Road
No Real Ale.

Queen of England ❽
54 Park Street
☎ (01753) 520476
11-3, 5-11; 11-11 (Fri, Sat); 12-10.30 (Sun)
Fuller's London Pride; Wadworth 6X; occasional guest beer Ⓗ
Comfortable, unpretentious backstreet local.

Red Cow ❾
140 Albert Street
☎ (01753) 522614
11-11; 12-10.30 (Sun)
Courage Best, Directors Ⓗ
Built as a farmhouse in 1547, now an oak-beamed two-bar pub. Mind your head coming in!

Rose & Crown ❿
312 High Street
☎ (01753) 521114
11-11; 12-10.30 (Sun)
Beer range varies Ⓗ
Excellent 17th-century hostelry which is a genuine free house offering at least two real ales at all times. First licensed in 1820. Mini beer festivals in summer. Karaoke Fri eve. Front patio and garden at rear. Sunday lunches, evening meals each night. *Recommended.*

Wheatsheaf ⓫
15 Albert Street
☎ (01753) 522019
11-11; 12-10.30 (Sun)
Fuller's Chiswick, London Pride, ESB, seasonal beers Ⓗ
Formerly a bakery but licensed as a pub in 1897. Small, comfortable one-bar pub with good local following of thirty-somethings. Red phone box in bar. Home-made pies flavoured with beer. Pool table. Occasional live music. *Recommended.*

Yates's Wine Lodge
277 High Street
No Real Ale.

Sonning F2

A charming and historic riverside village with its bridge and lock; a theatre/restaurant in an converted mill; some fine old houses and an attractive churchyard. The traffic over the bridge can be horrendous at times as it's a popular 'rat-run' between Caversham and the A4.

Bull

High Street (next to Sonning church, off B478)
☎ (0118) 969 3901
11-3, 5.30-11; 12-3, 7-10.30 (Sun); 12-10.30 (summer Sun)
Gales Butser, GB, HSB, seasonal beers Ⓗ

Attractive and historic pub near Sonning bridge, mainly given to serving food but with a separate area for drinkers. Pleasant patio and garden with a display of hanging baskets in summer. Accommodation is in the upper price bracket. The seasonal beers are served through a sparkler. *Recommended.*
🏰 ❀ 🛏 ◐ ◑ 🚂 P

French Horn

Sonning
No Real Ale.

Great House at Sonning Ferryman's Bar

Thames Street
☎ (0118) 969 2277
11-11; 12-10.30 (Sun)
Brakspear Bitter; **Fuller's** London Pride; **Wadworth** 6X Ⓗ

Large hotel on the Thames which is thought to date back to 13th century. Ferryman's Bar was the original ferryman's house before the bridge was built in 1790. Riverside bar and terrace. Meeting and conference rooms. Pricey but price lists displayed. *Recommended.*
Q ❀ 🛏 ◐ ◑ P

Speen C3

Hare & Hounds Hotel

Bath Road (A4)
☎ (01635) 521152
11-11; 12-10.30 (Sun)
Fuller's London Pride; **Arkell's** 3B; **Butts** Best; guest beer Ⓗ

Old coaching inn, now a hotel with bar and restaurant open to non-residents. Meals served every lunchtime and evening. Thirty rooms with en suite. *Recommended.*
Q ❀ 🛏 ◐ ◑ ♿ ♣ P

Starting Gate

75 Brummel Road, Speen
☎ (01635) 43859
11-11; 12-10.30 (Sun)
Fuller's London Pride; **Flower's** Original; **Boddingtons** Bitter; guest beer Ⓗ

Large one-bar estate pub with dining area. The name refers to the racecourse. Meals served every lunchtime and evening.

Spencers Wood F3

Farriers Arms

Basingstoke Road (B3349)
☎ (0118) 988 3132
11.30-3, 5.30-11 (6-11 Sat); 12-3, 7-10.30 (Sun)
Draught **Bass**; **Courage** Best, Directors; **Ruddles** County Ⓗ

Roadside pub with elongated lounge bar and award-winning garden. No children after 9. Smart dress only. Food mostly home cooked but on the pricey side. *Recommended.*
❀ ◐ ◑ P

'I would hate to be teetotal. Imagine waking in the morning to think that's the best you're going to feel all day'

Dean Martin

Bull,
Stanford Dingley

Stanford Dingley D3

Bull
(OS 576716)
☎ (0118) 974 4409
12-3 (not Mon), 7-11; 12-3, 7-10.30 (Sun)
West Berkshire Skiff, Goldstar, Good Old Boy; **Brakspear** Bitter Ⓗ
An excellent 15th-century village pub with a strong following for West Berkshire beers. Ring the Bull played and original wattle and daub wall visible in the Old Tap Room. Children welcome in the saloon bar until 8.30 (except Sat). Good quality menu. Plans to expand if local bureaucracy can be overcome. *Recommended.*
Q ❀ ◖◗ ♣ P

Old Boot
(OS 576714)
☎ (0118) 974 4292
11-3, 6-11; 12-3, 7-10.30 (Sun)
Brakspear Bitter, Special; **West Berkshire** Doctor Hexter's Wedding Ale; **Bateman** XXXB Ⓗ
Small bar fronts a side eating area and large conservatory at rear also set aside for diners. Huge garden at rear set in beautiful countryside is not to be missed. Large car park opposite. *Recommended.*
Q ❀ ◖◗ P

Stockcross B3

Tiny village west of Newbury, close to the controversial bypass.

Lord Lyon
Ermin Street (B4000, OS 433688)
☎ (01488) 608366
12-3, 6.30-11; 12-3, 6.30-10.30 (Sun)
Arkell's 2B, 3B Ⓗ
Smart and friendly village local named after a racehorse. During summer months, 2B is replaced with Arkell's seasonal beer. Food available 12–2, 7–9. *Recommended.*
❀ ◖◗ ♣ P

Rising Sun
Ermin Street (B4000)
☎ (01488) 608131
12-2 (2.30 Fri, Sat), 5.30 (6.30 Sat)-11; 12-3, 7-10.30 (Sun)
Ruddles Best, County Ⓗ
Locals' pub with much changed interior. Darts and pool played.

'Good ale, the true and proper drink of Englishmen.
He is not deserving of the name Englishman who speaketh against ale, that is a good ale'

George Henry Borrow (1803–1881)

Streatley D2

The village was once the location of the ancient fording place between the Berkshire Ridgeway and the Chiltern Icknield Way. There are attractive views from Streatley Hill, but sadly the old village stores (which offered a choice of over 150 different cheeses) has now closed. The railway station is across the river in Goring.

Bull at Streatley

Reading Road (A340/B4009)
☎ (01491) 872392
11.30-3, 6-11; 12-3, 7-10.30 (Sun)
Courage Best; Theakston's Old Peculier; Thomas Hardy Royal Oak, Pope's Traditional Ⓗ
Very pleasant and well-furnished old inn which now offers food, beer and accommodation. Recent refurbishment has enhanced the ambience and the friendly staff make visitors welcome. Handy for the Thames and local countryside. Food available all sessions and includes vegetarian menu. Four-poster beds available. *Recommended.*
P

Swan Diplomat Hotel

High Street (B4009)
☎ (01491) 873737
11-3, 5.30-11; 12-3, 7-10.30 (Sun)
Tetley Bitter Ⓗ
Beautifully located and very plush 4-star riverside hotel with small cocktail bar next to the restaurant. Expensive beer. Smart dress obligatory. Disabled access. Bar times extended for residents.

'When the hoary sage replied; 'Come my lad and drink some beer''

Dr Samuel Johnson (1709–1784)

Sunningdale J3

The A30 divides much of the village between Berkshire and Surrey and there are many large and impressive residences in this affluent area.

Nag's Head

28 High Street (off A30)
☎ (01344) 622725
12-3, 5-11; 12-11 (Fri, Sat); 12-10.30 (Sun)
Harvey's XX Mild, Pale Ale, BB, Old, Armada, seasonal beers Ⓗ
A welcome outpost for the Sussex brewer's beers. Two-bar pub with interesting cross-section of customers. Large garden. *Recommended.*
P

Royal Oak

19 Station Road (½ mile north of station)
☎ (01344) 623625
11-11; 12-10.30
Flowers Original; Ruddles County, Best Ⓗ
Small, comfortable backstreet local with splendid floral displays and large garden at rear. Popular for lunches.

Sunninghill H3

A large residential village, handy for Ascot, Windsor Park and Virginia Water.

Cannon

London Road (A329)
☎ (01344) 620456
11-3, 5.30-11; 11-11 (Sat); 12-10.30 (Sun)
Courage Best; Fuller's London Pride; guest beers Ⓗ
Two cannons guard the entrance to this small but friendly house with two distinctly separate drinking areas. One of several ex-Courage houses in the area to receive a new lease of life. Now in the ownership of Waverley Inns.

Carpenter's Arms
78 Upper Village Road (near B3020)
☎ (01344) 622763
11-3, 5-11; 11-11 (Fri, Sat); 12-10.30 (Sun)
Flowers Original; **Fuller's** London Pride; **Wadworth** 6X Ⓗ
Surprisingly large backstreet pub with a comfortable lounge divided into separate seating areas and a genuine public bar. Entertainments include quiz nights, Sky TV and karaoke. The Wethered's brewery mirror behind the bar gives a clue to the pub's origins.

Dog & Partridge
92 Upper Village Road (near B3020)
☎ (01344) 623204
11-4, 6-11; 11-11 (Sat); 12-10.30 (Sun)
Courage Best; **Fuller's** London Pride Ⓗ
One of three pubs in this village backstreet. This is the one for darts enthusiasts.

Duke's Head
2 Upper Village Road (near B3020)
☎ (01344) 626949
11-11; 12-10.30 (Sun)
Greene King IPA, Abbot, seasonal beers; **Marston's** Pedigree Ⓗ
A friendly local whose landlord takes a pride in looking after his cask ales. Three distinct drinking areas with children welcome in the no-smoking lounge off the front bar. Reasonably priced food from an interesting menu (not Sun eve). Not easy to find in the village backstreets but worth the effort. *Recommended.*

Old Belvedere Arms
London Road (A329)
☎ (01344) 621134
11.30-3, 5.30-11; 12-10.30 (Sun)
Flower's Original; **Boddingtons** Bitter; **Courage** Directors; **Young's** Special Ⓗ
Big pub on the edge of Windsor Great Park near Blacknest gate. Recently refurbished having previously been a Beefeater steakhouse although retains a similar style.

Three Jays
Sunninghill Road
Badly damaged by fire. Future uncertain.

Swallowfield F4

Crown
The Street
☎ (0118) 988 3260
11-3, 6-11; 12-3, 7-10.30 (Sun)
Morland Original; **Ruddles** Best, County Ⓗ
Large village local. Lively public bar with a pool table and a quieter lounge bar. *Recommended.*

George & Dragon
Church Road
☎ (0118) 988 4432
12-11; 12-3.30, 7-11 (Sun)
Adnams Bitter; **Fuller's** London Pride; **Wadworth** 6X Ⓗ
Pub/restaurant with a wine bar atmosphere to the east of the village. High class cuisine. *Recommended.*

Thatcham C3

An expanding small town in the Kennet Valley, with a busy little centre, a paper mill and some new industrial/business parks. The railway station and canaille are about a mile out of town.

Black Horse
St Johns Road (off A4)
☎ (01635) 862550
11-3, 7-11; 11-11 (Sat); 12-10.30 (Sun)
Courage Best, Directors; **Marston's** Pedigree Ⓗ
Community pub to the west of town centre, offering darts, pool and satellite TV.

Crickets
24 High Street
☎ (01635) 862113
Opening hours unavailable
Courage Best; Wadworth 6X; Greene King IPA; Fuller's London Pride Ⓗ
One-bar town pub with sporting theme despite losing the 'er' from its previous name, the Cricketers. In addition to own football and netball teams, plays host to Thatcham rugby and cricket clubs. Satellite sports TV. Lunches served every day except Mon. Eve meals Tue–Thur only.

Kings Head
59 The Broadway
☎ (01635) 862145
11-3, 6-11; 12-3, 7-10.30 (Sun)
Courage Best; Morland Old Speckled Hen Ⓗ
Old two-bar former coaching inn. Separate pool room. *Recommended.*
❀ 🛏 ◖ ◗ ⊞ ⇌ P

Mill House
Bradley-Moore Square, Dunston Park
☎ (01635) 867277
11-11; 12-10.30 (Sun)
Draught Bass; Worthington Bitter Ⓗ
Billed as a 'bar and family restaurant' with outside children's play area.

Old Chequers
36 Broadway
☎ (01635) 863312
Opening hours unavailable
Marston's Pedigree Ⓗ
Town centre pub with exposed timber beams and low ceilings. Partitioned into separate drinking areas. *Recommended.*
♔ ❀ ◖ ⇌ P

Plough
81 Chapel Street
☎ (01635) 860340
11-3, 6-11; 12-3, 6.30-10.30 (Sun)
Flowers Original; Fuller's London Pride Ⓗ
Two-bar local offering pub food and pool.

Swan
Station Road
☎ (01635) 862084
11-11; 12-10.30 (Sun)
Courage Best, Directors; Theakston XB Ⓗ
Large two-bar pub with partitioned-off games room and dining area.

Wheatsheaf
15 Chapel Street
☎ (01635) 862670
11-3, 5.30-11; 11-11 (Sat); 12-10.30 (Sun)
Archers Village; guest beers Ⓗ
Recently refurbished and extended town pub. Small public bar/games room and large lounge. Has recently converted to a free house. Small garden hosts barbecues in summer. Occasional live music. *Recommended.*
❀ 🛏 ⊞ ♣ P

White Hart
2 High Street
☎ (01635) 863251
11-11; 11-3, 7-11 (Sat); 12-3, 7-10.30 (Sun)
Courage Best; Wadworth 6X; Morland Old Speckled Hen Ⓗ
Comfortable one-bar inn with separate restaurant area. Lunches every day. Eve meals every day except Sun. Patio area. *Recommended.*
♔ Q ❀ 🛏 ◖ P

Theale E3

Known locally as The Ale – it was home to Blatch's Brewery, some of whose premises still stand next to The Bull. Today, there is a vast business park between the M4 and the station, but the village offers a good selection of pubs and beers.

Bull
41 High Street
☎ (0118) 930 3478
11-11; 12-10.30 (Sun)
Wadworth 6X, Henry's IPA Ⓗ
In spite of effort to create a homely atmosphere, this is essentially a young person's pub. Occupies part of former Blatch's Brewery. Live music nights.

Fox & Hounds, Sunnyside

Crown
2 Church Street (near A4)
☎ (0118) 930 2310
Flowers IPA; Wadworth 6X; West Berkshire Skiff Ⓗ
Built in 1710 and reputed to have been used as a brothel in 19th century. Nearest pub to Theale station. Large garden contains swings and an assault course. Although no price list displayed, prices are very reasonable. Lunches Mon–Fri 12–2. *Recommended.*
❀ ◐ ⇌

Falcon
31 High Street
☎ (0118) 930 2523
11-11; 12-10.30 (Sun)
Courage Best, Archers Best, occasional guest beers Ⓗ
Historic 16th-century coaching inn which is mainly unmodernised but tidy. Car park through archway. Good access for disabled but no special facilities. *Recommended.*
♨ ❀ ◐ ⊟ ♿ ⇌ P

Fox & Hounds
Station Road, Sunnyside
☎ (0118) 930 2295
11-3, 5-11; 11-3, 6-11 (Sat); 12-4, 7-10.30 (Sun)
Wadworth Henry's IPA, 6X, Farmer's Glory; guest beers Ⓗ
Large country pub close to Kennet & Avon canal. Up to five guest beers available. Popular with locals and nearby office workers. Good value food. Approx half mile from station. *Recommended.*
♨ ❀ ◐ ◑ ♿ ⇌ ♣ P

Lamb
22 Church Street
☎ (0118) 930 2216
12-3, 6-11; 12-10.30 (Sun)
Courage Best; guest beer Ⓗ
Recently extended family pub with relaxing lounge bar. Guest beer usually from West Berkshire Brewery. *Recommended.*
♨ Q ♞ ❀ ◐ ◑ ⊟ ♿ ⇌ P

Red Lion
5 Church Street
☎ (0118) 930 2394
12-11; 12-10.30 (Sun)
Ansells Bitter; Marston's Pedigree; guest beer Ⓗ
Cosy, friendly Victorian local with its own skittle alley. Guest beer comes from Tapster's Choice range. Close to Theale Station. *Recommended.*
♞ ◐ ◑ ♿ ⇌ ♣

Volunteer
65 Church Street
☎ (0118) 930 2489
12-3, 5.30-11; 12-3, 7-10.30 (Sun)
Fuller's Chiswick, London Pride, ESB Ⓗ
Bars knocked through to form one large and extended bar. Made cosy by low ceilings and mock beams. *Recommended.*
❀ ◐ ◑ ⇌ P

'What two ideas are more inseparable than Beer and Britannia?'

Rev. Sydney Smith (1771–1845)

Three Mile Cross F3

Swan
Basingstoke Road
☎ (0118) 988 3674
11-11; 12-3, 7-11 (Sat); 12-3, 7-10.30 (Sun)
Brakspear Special; **Courage** Best; **Wadworth** 6X, Henry's IPA; **Fuller's** London Pride; guest beer Ⓗ
Two lounge bars and small family dining room in old beamed building with inglenook, on old A33. Walking distance from M4 and Madejski stadium (Reading FC, etc). Pricey beer. Piano. Strong business lunch trade. Food at all times (limited menu 3–6). *Recommended.*
❀ ◐ ◑ P

Tidmarsh E2

Greyhound
The Street (A340)
☎ (0118) 984 3557
11-3, 5.30-11; 11-11 (Sat); 12-10.30 (Sun)
Brakspear Special; **Courage** Best; **Fuller's** London Pride; **Wadworth** 6X; **West Berkshire** Graft Ⓗ
Low-beamed, dimly lit, open-plan building with log fires, reputedly dating from 12th century. Restaurant at rear. Reopened within short time of serious fire which destroyed thatched roof in 1999. *Recommended.*
⌂ ❀ ◐ ◑ P

Tilehurst E3

The old village, with its pottery industry. has long been swallowed up by new housing and is now a large western suburb of Reading. It has good bus and rail services to town (the station is some distance from the village centre).

Bear
160 Park Lane
☎ (0118) 942 7328
11-11; 12-10.30 (Sun)
Courage Best Ⓗ
Lively pub, popular with the young. Alterations planned.

Beethovens
Oxford Road (A329)
☎ (0118) 942 7517
11-11; 12-10.30 (Sun)
Courage Best; **Wadworth** 6X; guest beer Ⓗ
Large hotel backing onto the Thames with its own mooring facilities. Built in 1882, although parts are older. Three beers are usually available in the pub but real beer is also served in the popular Bistro Cinq (booking recommended). Music in bar most weekends. Hotel has eleven rooms (three family). Formerly known as the Roebuck.

Berkshire Vintners Off Licence
33 Armour Road
☎ (0118) 942 5373
7-9; 12-9 (Sun)
Wadworth IPA; **Adnams** Broadside Ⓖ
Off licence with newsagent and lottery terminal. Large range of quality ports and wines. Take your own container for takeaway real ales.

Bird in Hand
14 Lower Armour Road
☎ (0118) 942 7065
11-3, 5.30-11; 12-3, 5.30-10.30 (Sun)
Courage Best; **Butts** Jester Ⓗ
Friendly local; one of two pubs in a small back-street! Jester is sometimes replaced with another beer from the Butts range.

Butchers Arms
9 Lower Armour Road
☎ (0118) 942 4313
11-3, 6-11; 12-3, 7-10.30 (Sun)
Flowers IPA; **Archers** Best Ⓗ
Basic but friendly locals' pub. Well worth a visit. *Recommended.*
❀ ⊞ ♿ ⇄ ♣ P

Fox & Hounds
116 City Road
☎ (0118) 942 2982
11-3, 6-11; 11-11 (Fri, Sat);
12-3, 7-10.30 (Sun)
Courage Best; guest beer Ⓗ
One of the old village pubs, now surrounded by housing: old photos show how it once looked. Cosy, well-furnished bar with games area to the rear. Bar meals available weekday lunchtimes and early eve.
Recommended.
❀◖◗♣P

Oak Tree
Spey Road
No Real Ale.

Plough
78 School Road
☎ (0118) 942 7250
11-11; 12-10.30 (Sun)
Marston's Pedigree; Tetley Bitter; guest beers Ⓗ
Large, down-to-earth one-bar pub popular with the young. Food available 12–3 Mon–Sat.

Prince of Wales
School Road
☎ (0118) 945 8931
12-11; 12-10.30 (Sun)
Draught Bass Ⓗ
Large, modern open-plan pub lacking in atmosphere.

Restoration
928 Oxford Road (A329)
☎ (0118) 942 7229
11-11; 12-10.30 (Sun)
Tetley Bitter Ⓗ
Thirties-style road house. Comfortable lounge open-plan into Mr Q's bar with TV sport and pool table.

Roundabout
Oxford Road (A329) (entrance via Rodway Road)
☎ (0118) 941 8922
11-11; 12-10.30 (Sun)
Boddingtons Bitter; Marston's Pedigree; Wadworth 6X Ⓗ
High above the roundabout on the busy Oxford Road. Familiar but pleasant Beefeater layout which includes a fairground roundabout horse.

Royal Oak
69 Westwood Glen
☎ (0118) 941 7300
11.30-11; 12-11 (Sat); 12-10.30 (Sun)
Ind Coope Burton Ale; Tetley Bitter; Greene King IPA Ⓗ
Nice old pub with lots of character, at the top of a very steep incline. No food Sun.
Recommended.
❀◖⊕P

Tylers Rest
149 Norcot Road
No Real Ale.

Victory
The Meadway
☎ (0118) 941 3162
12-11; 12-3.30, 6-10.30 (Sun)
Brakspear Special Ⓗ
Untypical Brakspear's house being a new estate pub adjacent to Meadway shopping precinct. Large, comfortable lounge with smaller public bar dominated by pool table. Named after Nelson's flagship and is decorated with many related mementoes. Live music and discos. Happy hour Wed 7–8. Garden at rear.

Touchen End H2

The name derives from two chains which marked the forest rides that met there (now replaced by roads). This was the location of the whipping post and the stocks – the mediaeval law of Windsor Forest!

Winagins Inn
Ascot Road (A330)
☎ (01628) 672529
11-3, 5-11; 12-3, 7-10.30 (Sun)
Marston's Bitter, Pedigree, seasonal beers Ⓗ
This is the third name adopted by this pub in the last decade and it is about to become a Greene King house, with several changes planned including adding accommodation, a pool room and a lounge. Beer range likely to change. Friendly and enthusiastic manager.
Recommended.
🛏◖◗♿P

Twyford G2

There were once no fewer than 22 pubs in the village during the heyday of the coaching trade! Latterly, Twyford has had connections with Benjamin Franklin and Alexander Pope, and was reputedly the wedding place of The Prince of Wales and Mrs Fitzherbert in 1785. Change at Twyford for trains to Henley.

Duke of Wellington

26 High Street (A3032)
☎ (0118) 934 0456
11.30-3, 5 (6 Sat)-11; 12-3, 7-10.30 (Sun)
Brakspear Bitter, Special, Old, Mild, Ⓗ
Deservedly popular 16th-century two-bar pub attracting a mixed clientele. Large garden suitable for children. Food menu limited. *Recommended.*
❀ ◖ ⊟ ≉ P

Golden Cross

38 Waltham Road (B3018)
☎ (0118) 934 0180
11-11; 12-3, 7-10.30 (Sun)
Brakspear Bitter, Fuller's London Pride, Greene King IPA Ⓗ
Attractive pub built in mid-19th century with two very distinct drinking areas. Noted for involvement with fund raising activities. One hundred yards from Twyford station. *Recommended.*
❀ ◖◗ ≉ P

J W Green's

25 London Road (A3032)
☎ (0118) 934 5016
11-11; 12-10.30 (Sun)
Whitbread Trophy Ⓗ
One-bar youth establishment with many TVs and loud juke box. Beer not always in good condition.

Waggon & Horses

61 High Street
☎ (0118) 934 0376
12-2.30, 5.30-11; 11-11 (Sat); 12-10.30 (Sun)
Courage Best, Greene King IPA Ⓗ
Flagged floors and low beams in split-level single bar.

Upper Basildon D2

Affluent village in pleasant rural setting.

Beehive

Aldworth Road
☎ (01491) 671269
11-2.30, 6.30-11; 11-11 (Sat); 12-10.30 (Sun)
Brakspear Bitter; West Berkshire Good Old Boy; guest beers Ⓗ
Unconventional but enthusiastically run pub with three contrasting seating areas from wooden seats and tables to settees with log fire. Separate smart restaurant. Outside drinking area includes gazebo. Guest beers usually from local breweries and change regularly. Check out the lava lamp on the bar. Food available most times except Sat afternoon (book weekends). *Recommended.*
❀ ◖◗ P

Red Lion

Aldworth Road
☎ (01491) 671234
12-2.30, 7-11; 12-2.30-7-10.30 (Sun)
Tetley Bitter Ⓗ
Rather neglected pub not helped by frequent changes of landlord. Beer garden and car park. Pool table.

Upper Bucklebury C3

Cottage Inn

26 Broad Lane
☎ (01635) 864544
11-3, 6-11; 12-2.30, 7-10.30 (Sun)
Ruddles Best; Marston's Pedigree Ⓗ
Comfortable village pub with separate dining area specialising in South African cuisine. No meals Sun or Mon eve. *Recommended.*
♔ Q ❀ ◖◗ ♣ P

Waltham St. Lawrence G2

A well-preserved village with attractive old buildings (including The Bell).

Bell

(near the church) near B3024
☎ (0118) 934 1788
11-3.30, 6-11; 12-3.30, 7-11 (Sun)
Brakspear Bitter; guest beers Ⓗ
Genuinely historic building built in about 1400 although first recorded as being used as a pub in 1723. Wonderful interior includes wooden fire-place and antique clock, and look out for the small room called the 'noggin'. Separate dining room displays a well which was discovered during floor renovations. No food Sun or Mon evenings. Usually at least three guest beers. *Recommended.*

Star

Broadmoor Road (B3024)
☎ (0118) 934 3486
11.30-2.30 (11-3 Sat), 6-11; 12-3, 7-10.30 (Sun)
Wadworth Henry's IPA, 6X; occasional guest beer Ⓗ
Small but comfortable village pub with separate restaurant area at back of bar. Most easterly of Wadworth's tied houses.

Warfield H3

The village is in danger of being swallowed up by Bracknell, but does retain its rural feel and incorporates several hamlets. The church is worth a visit.

Cricketers

Cricketers Lane (off B3034/3022)
☎ (01344) 882910
11-2.30, 6-11; 11-11 (Fri, Sat); 12-10.30 (Sun)
Greene King IPA, Triumph, Abbot, guest or seasonal beers Ⓗ
Attractive country pub which was once a hunting lodge in Windsor Forest. It has changed hands several times in recent years but is now owned by Suffolk brewers Greene King. Raised public bar has darts; three small lounge areas and a large restaurant at the rear. Being in a very rural setting, the pub offers a peaceful retreat from nearby Bracknell. Food 12–2, 6.30–9 (no food Sun eve). *Recommended.*
P

New Leathern Bottle

Jealotts Hill (A3095)
☎ (01344) 421282
12-11; 12-4, 7-10.30 (Sun)
Courage Best; **Brakspear** Bitter Ⓗ
Attractive traditional two-bar pub set back from the road. Public bar with tiled floor; lounge with pool table and TV. Children's play equipment and large garden at front. Bar meals 12–2 daily.

Plough & Harrow

Forest Road, Newell Green (A3095)
☎ (01344) 421021
12-2.30, 6-11; 11.30-11 (Fri-Sat); 12-10.30 (Sun)
Morland Independent IPA, Original, Tanner's Jack, Old Speckled Hen; **Adnams** Broadside; **Ruddles** Best; guest beer Ⓗ
A good mix of customers frequent this recently altered and refurbished pub which is handy for Bracknell and the new housing developments nearby. Excellent selection of ales with regular guest beer. Sports TV and piped music. Usually seven beers available: well worth a visit. *Recommended.*
P

'I always keep a supply of stimulant handy in case I see a snake – which I also keep handy'

W.C. Fields

Shepherd's House
Moss Hill (A3095)
☎ (01344) 423341
11-11; 12-11 (Sun)
Courage Best; Theakston Best; guest beer Ⓗ
Restaurant and lounge bar with games area. Large function room/ conference area. Extensively rebuilt in 1998. *Recommended.*
◐ P

Three Legged Cross
Forest Road (A3095)
☎ (01344) 421673
11-3, 5.30 (6 Sat)-11; 12-3, 7-10.30 (Sun)
Courage Best, Directors; Marston's Pedigree Ⓗ
Cosy old building with all rooms knocked into one. Small garden by stream. Food lunchtimes Mon–Sat. *Recommended.*
❀ P

Yorkshire Rose
Forest Road, Newell Green (A3095)
☎ (01344) 483672
12-3, 6-11; 12-3 (Sun)
Courage Best; Theakston Best, XB Ⓗ
A small bar at the front of an à la carte restaurant with an extensive menu. Bar meals also available. Food 12–2.15, 6–10 (closed Sun eve). *Recommended.*
Q ❀ ◐ P

Wargrave G2

A Thames-side village which has retained much of its charm and character. The name means 'the grove of trees by the weir'. Madame Tussaud is interred in the churchyard and Emma – the mother of Edward the Confessor – once had a palace here to which she was 'retired' after helping murder Edward's brother and plotting to do away with the rest of her family!

Bull
High Street (A321)
☎ (0118) 940 3120
12-2.30, 6-11; 12-2.30, 6-10.30 (Sun)
Brakspear Bitter, Special, seasonal beers Ⓗ
Very attractive old inn located on crossroads in centre of village. Real wooden beams and many horse brasses plus a welcoming fire in winter. Good value food with interesting menu. *Recommended.*
Q ❀ ◐ ≠

Greyhound
79 High Street (A321)
☎ (0118) 940 2556
11-11; 12-10.30 (Sun)
Courage Best; guest beer Ⓗ
Nice old two-bar pub on the same crossroads as the Bull. Lunches available until 2. Guest beer changes regularly. Small car park.

St George & Dragon
Henley Road (A321)
☎ (0118) 940 3852
12-3, 6-11; 12-11 (Sat); 12-10.30 (Sun)
Draught Bass; Worthington Bitter Ⓗ
Uninspired Harvester restaurant with patio doors to terrace and garden with a few benches offering river views. May move to all day opening.

White Hart
High Street (A321)
☎ (0118) 940 2590
11-3, 6-11; 12-3, 6-10.30 (Sun)
Fuller's London Pride; Wadworth 6X; Whitbread Best; Brakspear Bitter Ⓗ
Small village hotel with old-fashioned but comfortable lounge bar. Separate restaurant with good quality menu available from 7 (not Sun). Large car park at rear.

'St George he was for England, and before he killed the dragon
He drank a pint of English Ale out of an English flagon'

G.K. Chesterton (1874–1936)

Warren Row G2

Crooked Inn
Warren Row Road
☎ (01628) 825861
11.30-2.30, 5.30-11; 11.30-3 (Sun/closed eve)
Brakspear Bitter Ⓗ
Previously 'Old House at Home' then 'Frog & Toad', now a good quality restaurant with only a small area for non-dining drinkers.

Wash Common C4

The site of the first Battle of Newbury in 1643 – a fact commemorated by a memorial opposite the pubs. (The inscription to Viscount Falkland is written in Latin and Greek as well as English for some reason.)

Gun
142 Andover Road (A343)
☎ (01635) 47292
11-11; 12-10.30 (Sun)
Courage Best, Directors; Theakston XB Ⓗ
Comfortable two-bar community pub on the outskirts of Newbury offering the best priced beer in town. Nearest rail station: Newbury. *Recommended.*
❀ ◐ ◑ ⊟ ⇌ P

Old Bell
215 Andover Road (A343)
No Real Ale.

Wash Water C4

Woodpecker
(off A343, OS 452635)
☎ (01635) 43027
11-2.30, 5.45-11; 12-3, 6.30-10.30 (Sun)
Arkell's 2B, 3B, Kingsdown Ⓗ
Comfortable one-bar pub with separate dining area, specialising in B&B accommodation and Sunday roast – without tripping over children! *Recommended.*
Q ⛟ ◐ ◑ P

Water Oakley J2

Queen's Head
Windsor Road (A308)
☎ (01628) 633781
11.30-3, 5.30-11; 12-3.30 (Sun)
Greene King IPA; Tetley Bitter; guest beer Ⓗ
Small 16th-century road pub. Tapas menu 12–2.30, 6–10 (Sun lunchtime only). New management; details may change.

West Ilsley C1

John Morland bought a maltings in the village in 1711 which was the beginning of the family brewing business that later transferred to Abingdon.

Harrow
(near A34, OS 471826)
☎ (01635) 281260
11-3, 6-11; 12-4, 7-10.30 (Sun)
Morland Original, Old Speckled Hen; Flower's Original Ⓗ
Attractive village pub in horse country, opposite cricket pitch and duck pond. Single bar where you are as likely to be shoulder to shoulder with a stable lad or one of the Queen's trainers. Tables in front of pub in unusual steep garden on side of downs. Good food but a bit pricey. Close to Ridgeway path. *Recommended.*
♔ Q ❀ ◐ ◑

White Waltham G2

Small village with an airfield for private planes.

Beehive
Waltham Road
☎ (01628) 822877
11-2.30, 5.30-11; 12-3, 7-10.30 (Sun)
Brakspear Bitter; Flowers IPA, Original; guest beer Ⓗ
Thriving, friendly two-bar local overlooking cricket pitch. Car park has recently been extended reducing the size of the garden. *Recommended.*
❀ ◐ ◑ ⊟ ♣ P

Wickham B3

Situated in the Lambourn Valley, the village church has some interesting and unusual features (you'll have to visit to find out what!)

Five Bells

Baydon Road (OS 394718)
☎ (01488) 608242
12-3, 6-11; 12-3, 7-10.30 (Sun)
Ringwood Best Bitter; Fuller's London Pride; Flowers Original Ⓗ; **occasional guest cider** Ⓖ
Sixteenth-century thatched village inn with large garden. Comfortable bar with adjoining dining area serving excellent food. Lunchtime meals every day. Eve meals every day except Sun. *Recommended.*
⛫ Q ❀ ⛟ ◐ ◑ ♿ ⛾ P

Windsor J2

World famous for its Castle, it is a must on the tourist route, but can get very frenetic in the summer months, when you can spot just about every make of camera and hear almost every language being spoken. The pubs around the centre cater, naturally, for the tourist trade but there are several good local boozers away from the main attractions. Windsor also has the Great Park; a riverside racecourse; an excellent theatre; boat trips; Legoland and the pedestrian footbridge over the Thames to Eton.

The Windsor breweries have long gone and most of the pubs are supplied by the big combines and larger independents. Windsor's two stations can get you to London Waterloo or to Paddington via Slough.

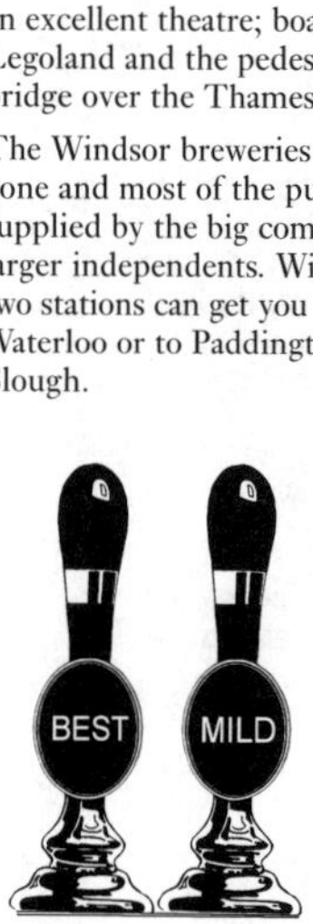

Adam & Eve ❶

29 Thames Street
☎ (01753) 864359
11-11; 12-10.30 (Sun)
Draught Bass Ⓗ
Small beamed pub opposite the castle and convenient for Windsor Theatre. Occasional karaoke and calypso nights.

Alma ❷

61 Springfield Road
☎ (01753) 862641
Opening hours unavailable
Tetley Bitter Ⓗ
Backstreet Victorian local named after Crimean battle of 1854.

Bell

2 Dedworth Road, Clewer (B3024)
☎ (01753) 861867
Opening hours unavailable
Courage Best; John Smith's Bitter Ⓗ
Small local pub.

Bexley Arms ❸

Bexley Street
☎ (01753) 865552
11-11; 12-10.30 (Sun)
Courage Best; guest beer Ⓗ
Edge of town centre pub with horseshoe-shaped bar.

Black Horse

290 Dedworth Road, Dedworth (B3024)
☎ (01753) 861953
11-3, 5-11; 11-11 (Sat); 12-10.30 (Sun)
Ind Coope Burton; Fuller's London Pride; Adnams Bitter Ⓗ
Comfortable one-bar locals' pub. Food weekday lunchtimes only. Occasional live music and discos. *Recommended.*
⛫ ❀ ◐ P

Bricklayer's Arms

Hatch Lane
☎ (01753) 863531
12-11; 12-10.30 (Sun)
Courage Best Ⓗ
Two-bar local off the beaten track.

Café Rouge

Royal Station Concourse
No Real Ale.

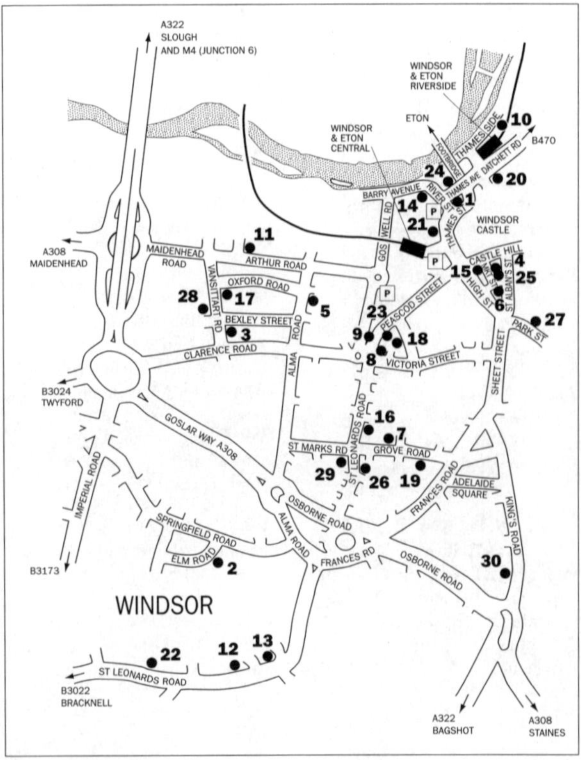

Carpenter's Arms ❹

4 Market Street
☎ (01753) 755961
11-11; 12-10.30 (Sun)
Draught Bass; Worthington Best Ⓗ
Interesting pub built circa 1518. Seating is around square central bar. Situated in the touristy part of town near the castle. Opens 11 Sun for breakfast.

Chicago Rock Café

William Street
No Real Ale.

Copper Horse ❺

7 Ward Royal Parade, Alma Road
☎ (01753) 869379
12-11; 12-10.30 (Sun)
John Smith's Bitter Ⓗ
Sixties vintage, two-bar pub frequented by locals. Low ceilings lead to very smoky atmosphere at times.

Corner Bar

22 Sheet Street
No Real Ale.

Court Jester ❻

Church Lane
☎ (01753) 864257
12-11; 12-10.30 (Sun)
Tetley Bitter; Ind Coope Burton Ale; guest beers Ⓗ
Oldish pub, now a Festival Ale House which was redesigned in 1998. In the tourist area with prices to match. Four guest beers usually available. Beer quality can be variable.

Crispin ❼

56 Grove Road
☎ (01753) 865517
11-11; 12-10.30 (Sun)
Courage Best; guest beer Ⓗ
Grade II listed community local. The prices are the same in both bars but they are definitely public and saloon. Separate pool room. Food 12–3 every day.

Criterion ❽
72 Peascod Street
☎ (01753) 866139
11–11; 12–10.30 (Sun)
Brakspear Special; Courage Best Ⓗ
Small, early 19th-century pub on main shopping street with windows promoting Ashby's Staines brewery (closed 1931). Mainly locals but very friendly. Pavement seats in summer. No lunches Sun. *Recommended.*
❀ ◖ ≹

Crosses Corner ❾
73 Peascod Street
☎ (01753) 862867
11–11; 12–10.30 (Sun)
Courage Best Ⓗ
Wine bar on edge of town centre.

Donkey House ❿
10 Thames Side
☎ (01753) 860644
11–11; 12–10.30 (Sun)
Marston's Pedigree; Morland Old Speckled Hen; Tetley Bitter Ⓗ
Riverside pub, nicely refurbished early 1999. Sit outside and wave at the river traffic or sit inside and laugh at those waving outside. Children welcome inside until 7.30 then it's over 20s only. Extensive menu available 12–9 Mon–Fri, 12–7 Sat, Sun. Australians particularly welcome! *Recommended.*
❀ ◖◗ ≹ P

Duke of Connaught ⓫
165 Arthur Road
☎ (01753) 865211
11–11; 12–10.30 (Sun)
Greene King IPA, Abbot; guest beer Ⓗ
Locals' pub on edge of town centre named after Queen Victoria's third son.

Duke of York ⓬
198 St Leonards Road (B3022)
☎ (01753) 864515
Opening hours unavailable
Ushers Best, Founders Ⓗ
Real ale not always available in this single-bar locals' pub.

Fawn ⓭
140 St Leonards Road (B3022)
☎ (01753) 861203
11-11; 12-10.30 (Sun)
Tetley Bitter Ⓗ
Two-bar community local.

Fort & Firkin ⓮
River Street
☎ (01753) 869897/861043
11-11; 12-10.30 (Sun)
Firkin Royale, Best, Fort Ale, Dogbolter, Porter Ⓗ
Large, extended, street corner pub overlooking the Thames. Unlike a number of Firkin pubs, this one actually brews its own beers: brewery visible in corner of bar. At Christmas Winter Warmer replaces porter.

Harte & Garter
High Street
No Real Ale.

Horse & Groom ⓯
Castle Hill
☎ (01753) 830172
10.30-11; 11-10.30 (Sun)
Courage Best, Directors Ⓗ
Lovely little pub by castle gates. Bar staff are multi-lingual by necessity.

Maypole
Dedworth Road, Dedworth (B3024)
☎ (01753) 862688
11-11; 12-3, 7-10.30 (Sun)
Draught Bass; Fuller's London Pride Ⓗ
Large pub renovated, again, in late 1998. Previously the Dedworth Arms but still known locally by its original name, the Wolf.

Merry Wives ⓰
65 St Leonards Road
☎ (01753) 861860
Opening hours unavailable
Greene King Abbot Ⓗ
One-bar pub extensively modernised in recent years.

Mitre ⓱
Oxford Road
☎ (01753) 862510
11-11; 12-10.30 (Sun)
Fuller's London Pride Ⓗ
Locals' pub whose owner/licensee takes great pride in the standard of his real ale. Around twenty teams operate from here, varying from crib to clay pigeon shooting. Food 12–2.30, 6–9 Mon–Sat. *Recommended.*
◐◑♣

Olde King & Castle
Thames Street
Real Ale in cellar bar only but closed for refurbishment at time of survey.

Old Monk ⓲
11 William Street
☎ (01753) 855531
11-11, 12-10.30 (Sun)
Theakston Best; guest beers Ⓗ
Large new pub opened in 1998. Operated by Old Monk Co. set up by the brother of Wetherspoon's founder and run along similar lines but with music. Five guest beers usually available.

Old Ticket Hall Wine Bar
Windsor & Eton Riverside Station, Datchet Road
No Real Ale.

Prince Albert
2 Clewer Hill Road
☎ (01753) 864788
11-11; 12-10.30 (Sun)
Courage Best; Marston's Pedigree Ⓗ
Cosy two-bar pub, named after the Prince Consort, near Legoland. Once a hunting lodge.

Prince Arthur ⓳
29 Grove Road
☎ (01753) 861779
11-11; 12-10.30 (Sun)
Flowers Original Ⓗ
Modernised backstreet pub with splendid tiled exterior. Extensive menu, predominantly Thai, available 12.30–9.30 Mon, Wed, Thur, Sun and 12.30–10.30 Fri, Sat.

Punters Wine Bar
Thames Street
No Real Ale.

Queen
382 Dedworth Road, Dedworth (B3024)
☎ (01753) 675248
11-3, 5-11; 11-11 (Fri, Sat); 12-10.30 (Sun)
Morland Original; Ruddles Best; guest beer Ⓗ
Comfortable one-bar pub in western suburb. Live MOR music, usually Wed. Quiz nights. Petanque played. Family room. Food available 12–2, 6–9.30. *Recommended.*
P

Royal Adelaide Hotel
Kings Road
No Real Ale.

Royal Oak ⑳
Datchet Road (B470)
☎ (01753) 865179
11-11; 12-10.30 (Sun)
Courage Best, Directors; Wadworth 6X Ⓗ
Pleasant half-timbered pub, replete with beams, dados and stained glass. Separate eating area. Convenient for Riverside station.

Salvana Wine Bar
Charles Street
No Real Ale.

Sebastopol
Clewer Hill Road, Dedworth
☎ (01753) 620870
11-11; 12-10.30 (Sun)
Morland Original, Tanner's Jack; Ruddles Best Ⓗ
Fairly plush one-bar pub at the apex of Clewer Hill. Named after seaport under siege during Crimean War.

'Did you ever taste beer?'
'I had a sip of it once'
said the small servant.
'Here's a state of things!
cried Mr Swiveller...
'She never tasted it – it
can't be tasted in a sip'

Charles Dickens (1812–1859)
'The Old Curiosity Shop'

Shooters Bar & Diner
Goswell Road
No Real Ale.

Slug & Lettuce ㉑
High Street
☎ (01753) 864405
11-11; 12-10.30 (Sun)
Shepherd Neame Spitfire, Masterbrew; Courage Best Ⓗ
After several refurbishments and two name changes, the Knights Tavern has now become a modern café bar. Nice place but lacks traditional pub atmosphere.

Stag & Hounds ㉒
302 St Leonards Road
☎ (01753) 861986
11-3, 6-11; 11-11 (Sat); 12-10.30 (Sun)
Courage Best; Wadworth 6X Ⓗ
Two-bar 16th-century pub.

Star ㉓
51 Peascod Street
☎ (01753) 755951
11-11; 12-10.30 (Sun)
Draught Bass Ⓗ
Large pub on Windsor's main shopping street.

Swan ㉔
49 Thames Street
☎ (01753) 861794
11-11; 12-10.30 (Sun)
Courage Best Ⓗ
Small, basic one-bar pub at the Windsor end of Eton bridge. Available beer likely to change.

Swan
9 Mill Lane, Clewer Village (off A308)
☎ (01753) 862069
12-3, 6-11; 12-2, 6-11 (Sat); 12-3, 7-10.30 (Sun)
Flowers IPA, Original; Fuller's London Pride Ⓗ
Little 16th-century pub reputedly having tunnels to the castle and a ghost. Kitchen was once a mortuary. YHA camping nearby. Accommodation comprises seven rooms. *Recommended.*
Δ ♣ P

Three Elms
Clarence Road, Clewer (B3024)
☎ (01753) 864344
11-2.30, 4.30-11; 11-11 (Fri, Sat); 12-10.30 (Sun)
Morland Original; Ruddles County Ⓗ
Local with several drinking areas.

Three Tuns ㉕
8 Market Street
☎ (01753) 861615
11-11; 12-10.30 (Sun)
Courage Best, Directors Ⓗ
Pleasant pub on a cobbled street in the tourist part of town.

Trooper ㉖
97 St Leonards Road
☎ (01753) 670123
12-11; 12-6 (Sun)
Theakston Best; Brakspear Special Ⓗ
Pleasant one-bar pub.

Two Brewers ㉗
34 Park Street
☎ (01753) 855426
11-11; 12-10.30 (Sun)
Courage Best; Wadworth 6X; Marston's Pedigree Ⓗ
Small two-bar pub by gate to Long Walk. Collection of wine corks.

Vansittart Arms ㉘
105 Vansittart Road
☎ (01753) 865988
11-11; 12-10.30 (Sun)
Fuller's London Pride, ESB, seasonal beers Ⓗ
Excellent old pub hidden in back street just off town centre. Very popular for both eating and drinking. No food Sun eve. *Recommended.*
❀ ◑

Windsor Arts Centre ㉙
The Old Court, St Leonards Road
☎ (01753) 859421
7.30-11; 12-10 (Sun)
Fuller's London Pride, seasonal beers; guest beer Ⓗ
Once a fire station. Clientele tend to reflect the show or event currently on. Bar is staffed by volunteers, hence the opening hours. Acoustic musician live in the bar Wed, Sun. Disabled access at rear and disabled toilet available. *Recommended.*
♿ ⇌ P

Windsor Castle ㉚
98 Kings Road
☎ (01753) 858977
12-11; 12-10.30 (Sun)
Courage Best; Brakspear Bitter Ⓗ
One-bar pub overlooking the Great Walk. One of numerous pubs in the land to bear this name but this one is actually in sight of its namesake. Occasional discos, etc.

Windsor Lad
250 Maidenhead Road (A308)
☎ (01753) 864634
12-11; 12-10.30 (Sun)
Worthington Best Bitter; Fuller's London Pride Ⓗ
Large, plush Harvester steakhouse next to Windsor racecourse.

'Would I were in an alehouse in London! I would give all my fame for a pot of ale and safety'

William Shakespeare (1564–1616)

Winkfield H3

A scattered community which includes Cranbourne, Maidens Green and Woodside. Ascot racecourse and Windsor Great Park are close by.

Cottage Inn
Winkfield Street, Maidens Green (off B3022)
☎ (01344) 882242
12-3, 6-11; closed Sun eve
Greene King IPA, Abbot Ⓖ
High-class restaurant in old pub building with flagged floors. Small bar area; excellent beer. Gets crowded; booking advised. Food available until 9.45.
Recommended.
Q P

Crispin
Windsor Road (A332/B3034)
☎ (01344) 882164
11-11, 12-10.30 (Sun)
Morland Original, Old Speckled Hen; Ruddles County Ⓗ
Large roadside pub named after the patron saint of cobblers, near to Windsor Great Park. Recently refurbished with fake wooden beams. Morland Artist's Fare food menu.

Crown & Anchor
Maidens Green (B3022)
☎ (01344) 882829
11-3, 5.30-11; 12-4 (Sun)
Morland Original Ⓗ
Bright and pleasant lounge bar with conservatory and patio. Closed Sun evenings. (Recently changed hands when surveyed so opening hours may change.)
Recommended.
P

Fleur De Lys
Hatchet Lane (A330)
☎ (01344) 882295
12-3, 6 (varies)-11; 11-11 (Sat); 12-10.30 (Sun)
Ruddles Best, County; Morland Original; guest beers Ⓗ
Basic, street corner locals' pub. Guest beer comes from Morland standard range.

Herne's Oak
North Street (B3022)
☎ (01344) 882940
12-2, 5-11; 12-4, 7-11 (Sat); 12-6, 8-10.30 (Sun)
Brakspear Bitter; Boddingtons Bitter; Marston's Pedigree Ⓗ
Small two-roomed pub with strong Chelsea FC theme. Herne was a mythical king's hunter whose ghost is said to appear at a great oak tree in Windsor Forest. Closed Mon lunchtime.

Old Hatchet
Hatchet Lane (A330)
☎ (01344) 885545
11-11, 12-10.30 (Sun)
Draught Bass; guest beer Ⓗ
Attractive Grade II listed country pub originally converted from three cottages. Currently undergoing changes as part of 're-branding' as a Vintage Inn by owners Bass.

White Hart, Winkfield

Squirrels
North Street (B3022)
☎ (01344) 882205
11-11; 12-10.30 (Sun)
Courage Best, Directors Ⓗ
Large single bar with dining area. Dominated by large screen TV which appears to be constantly on! Popular with the very young. Pool table.

Stirrups
Maidens Green (A330)
☎ (01344) 882284
11-11; 12-10.30 (Sun)
Courage Best, Directors Ⓗ
Smart bar incorporated into large plush country house hotel with 24 bedrooms and conference facilities. Private function facilities for up to 150 people. Bar meals available lunchtimes and evenings. Four executive suites recently added. Large car park.

White Hart
Church Road (A330)
☎ (01344) 882415
11-3, 6-11; 12-3, 7-10.30 (Sun)
Courage Best, Fuller's London Pride; Rebellion Smuggler Ⓗ
Well-kept old building which was a small courthouse and gaol in 16th century. Meals available in lounge bar or separate restaurant with its real fires, one a large inglenook. Car park at rear or parking in front of church opposite. *Recommended.*
⛫ Q ❀ ◖◗

Winkfield
11 Lovell Road (A330)
☎ (01344) 883498
11-3, 6-11; 12-10.30 (Sun)
Fuller's London Pride; Brakspear Bitter; Flowers Original; guest beer Ⓗ
Small, comfortable, up-market bar at the front of a large restaurant area. Guest beer changes regularly. Previously called the Slug & Lettuce.

Winnersh F3

Mainly residential but there is a new business park and multiplex cinema near to Winnersh Triangle station.

Pheasant
355 Reading Road (A329)
☎ (0118) 978 4529
11-11, 12-10.30 (Sun)
Courage Best, Directors; guest beer Ⓗ
Pub with twelve-room hotel attached. The large bar is very lively and can be noisy. MTV screens. Amongst the huge collection of paraphernalia is an interesting display of cigarette cards. Business breakfast available. Petanque terrain (boules pitch) at rear.

Wheelwrights Arms
Davis Way, Davis Street (off B3030 opp. Dinton Pastures Country Park entrance)
☎ (0118) 934 4100
11.30-2.30, 5.30-11; 11.30-11 (Sat); 12-10.30 (Sun)
Wadworth IPA, 6X, Badger Tanglefoot; seasonal beers Ⓗ
Medium-sized country pub with character. One large bar with open fires and plenty of seating. Separate eating area. *Recommended.*
Q ❀ ◖◗ ♿ P ⍻

Winterbourne C3

Winterbourne Arms
(OS 455722)
☎ (01635) 248200
11.30-3, 6-11; 12-4 (Sun)
Flowers Original; Brakspear Bitter; West Berkshire Good Old Boy Ⓗ
Large village pub formerly known as the New Inn. Central bar is flanked by areas set aside for food. Extensive menu available. Closed Sun eve. *Recommended.*
⛫ Q ❀ ◖◗ P

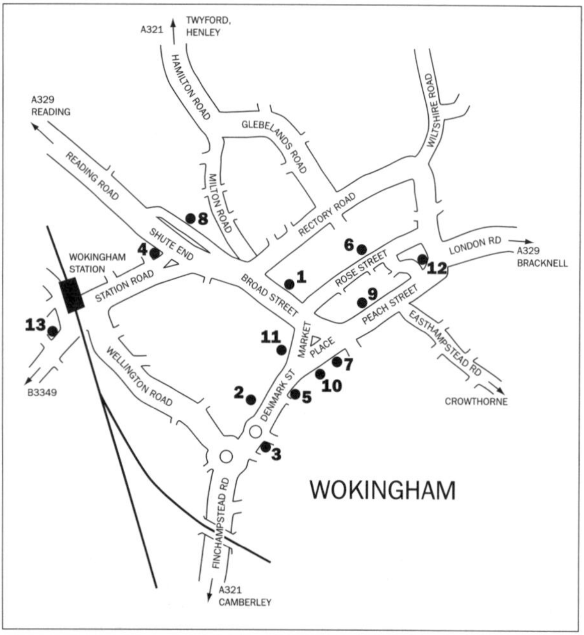

Wokingham G3

A 700-year-old market town which still retains a little of its old character (Broad Street and The Terrace being good examples). The town encompasses Emmbrook and Wokingham Without although the area controlled by the local council is scattered far and wide. The beer choice is not bad with local and regional brewers represented alongside the more national products. There are good rail connections to Reading, London and Gatwick.

Big Hand Mo's
59 Station Road
No Real Ale.

Broad Street Tavern ❶
29 Broad Street
☎ (0118) 977 3706
11-11; 12-10.30 (Sun)
Wadworth IPA, 6X, Summersault, seasonal beers; guest beers Ⓖ/Ⓗ
Large multi-roomed pub with central bar. Located in the town centre, this welcoming house has a garden accessible through the bar. Regular special events include music evenings and mini beer festivals. *Recommended.*
❀ ◗ ⚡

Bullfinch
Forest Road (B3034)
☎ (01344) 304446
11-11; 12-10.30 (Sun)
Draught Bass; Fuller's London Pride Ⓗ
Former Warren Inn reopened June 1999 after a major conversion into comfortable but routine Vintage Inns formula. Country house effect uses deliberately mismatched wooden chairs. Food served at most times from standard menu. Stupid pub sign shows a finch's body with a bull's head!

Crispin ❷
45 Denmark Street A321
☎ (0118) 978 0309
Brakspear Bitter; Wadworth 6X Ⓗ
Town centre pub comprising one bar with mainly young clientele. Juke box – good atmosphere. 6X served through handpump with sparkler.

Crooked Billet
Honey Hill (off Nine Mile Ride)
☎ (0118) 978 0438
11-11; 12-10.30 (Sun)
Brakspear Bitter, Special, seasonal beers Ⓗ
Superb country pub situated 1½ miles to south-east of town centre. The unspoilt bar has a welcoming fire in winter. There is a small restaurant area and look out for the small 'snug' by the dartboard. Beware of the ford if approaching from the north-east! *Recommended.*
⛰ Q ❀ ◖◗ ♿ ♣ P

Dog & Duck
Matthews Green Road, Emmbrook (near A329)
☎ (0118) 978 0544
11.30-2.30, 5.30-11; 12-11 (Sat); 12-10.30 (Sun)
Brakspear Bitter, Special Ⓗ
Comfortable suburban local. The original building sports typical Brakspear's painted signs, but has been much extended. Separate eating area.

Duke's Head ❸
56 Denmark Street (A321)
☎ (0118) 978 0316
11.30-3, 5.30 (5 Fri, 6 Sat)-11; 12-3, 7-10.30 (Sun)
Brakspear Bitter, Special, seasonal beers Ⓗ
Lively and popular town pub with its own skittle alley. Good lunches (not Sun) and a splendid hanging flower basket display in summer. No-smoking area lunchtimes only. *Recommended.*
Q ❀ ◖ ≹ ♣ P ⊬

Hope & Anchor ❹
11 Station Road
☎ (0118) 978 0918
11-2.30, 5-11; 11-11 (Fri, Sat); 12-10.30 (Sun)
Brakspear Bitter, Special, seasonal beers; **Boddingtons** Bitter Ⓗ
Lively town pub with skittle alley and function room popular with all generations. Occasional quiz nights. Food available 12–2 (Mon–Thur), 12–3 (Fri–Sun) and 5.30–8.30 every evening. *Recommended.*
◖◗ ≹ ♣

Lord Raglan ❺
30 Denmark Street
☎ (0118) 962 9007/978 0455
12-11; 7-10.30 (Sun)
Morland Bitter; **Ruddles** Bitter Ⓗ
Victorian town centre pub knocked through to one bar. Younger clientele (football etc). Ruddles served through a sparkler.

Metropolitan ❻
56 Rose Street
☎ (0118) 978 1171
11-11; 12-10.30 (Sun)
Morland Original; **Ruddles** Bitter Ⓗ
Town centre, side street local. Bar & 'Glass & Pewter' lounge.

Crooked Billet, Wokingham

Norreys Barn
Ashridge Road (off Wiltshire Rd)
☎ (0118) 961 9361
12-11; 12-10.30 (Sun)
Morland Original; Flowers Original Ⓗ
Nineteen-fifties/sixties estate local with separate bar & lounge. Darts played. Locals very pally. A good example of the genre.

Olde Rose Inn ❼
Market Place
☎ (0118) 978 0130
11-11; 12-10.30 (Sun)
Marston's Pedigree; Boddington Bitter; Wadworth 6X Ⓗ
Old coaching inn, but much refurbished; now in typical Beefeater style. Very busy haunt of the very young. Typical drink is 'Heineken Top'. Looks like the in-place of the moment. All beers dispensed through swan necks and tight sparklers.

Olde Leathern Bottel
221 Barkham Road (B3349)
☎ (0118) 978 4222
11-11, 12-10.30 (Sun)
Courage Best, Directors; Theakston XB Ⓗ
Large food-orientated pub. Busy with mainly young clientele. All beers not always available.

Plough
London Road (A329)
☎ (0118) 978 9677
11-11; 12-10.30 (Sun)
Morland Original, Old Speckled Hen; Ruddles Best Ⓗ
Large steakhouse and pub, reopened April 1999 after refurbishment. Outdoor drinking area. Good-sized car park and close to A329(M). Food available 12–10. *Recommended.*
❀ ◐ ◑ P

Queen's Head ❽
23 The Terrace (near A329)
☎ (0118) 978 1221
11-2.30, 5.30-11; 12-3, 5.30-11 (Sun)
Morland Independent IPA, Original; Ruddles County; seasonal beers Ⓗ
Standing on magnificent terrace overlooking Station and Reading roads, this quintessential English pub is one of Wokingham's oldest. Compact bar and discreet walled garden. Darts and Aunt Sally pitch. *Recommended.*
❀ ◐ ≉ ♣

Redan ❾
24 Peach Street
☎ (0118) 978 6817
11-11; 3-10.30 (Sun)
Morland Independent IPA, Original Ⓗ
Located in the busy Peach Street, this large single-bar pub has a big patio garden. Named after a type of trench used in the Crimean War. Regular music evenings.

Red Lion ❿
25 Market Place
☎ (0118) 978 0319
11-3, 5.30-11; 12-3, 7-10.30 (Sun)
Brakspear Bitter, Special Ⓗ
Two-bar pub decorated with a large collection of bric-a-brac and interesting old prints. Popular Thai restaurant upstairs. *Recommended.*
◐ ◑ ≉ P

Rifle Volunteer
141 Reading Road (A329)
☎ (0118) 978 4484
11-2.30, 5.30-11; 11-11 (Sat); 12-5.30, 7-10.30 (Sun)
Courage Best, Directors Ⓗ
Knocked-through one-bar local, out of town centre.

Roebuck ⓫
8 Market Place
☎ (0118) 978 0810
11-11; 12-10.30 (Sun)
Flowers Original; Courage Best Ⓗ
Small town centre pub situated in pedestrianised area. Pool table and small garden at rear. All day breakfast.

Ship ⓬
104–108 Peach Street
☎ (0118) 978 0389
12-3, 5-11 (Mon-Thur); 12-11 (Fri, Sat); 12-10.30 (Sun)
Fuller's Chiswick, London Pride, ESB, seasonal beers; guest beers Ⓗ
Two-bar split-level pub decorated with much movie memorabilia. A drinking vessel displayed in the left-hand bar is inscribed 'Ship Inn, Oakingham, Wilts'. The pub is located a few feet away from the boundary stone marking the old Berks/Wilts border. Evening meals cease at 8 Sun, 9 Mon–Thur and not available Fri/Sat. *Recommended.*
❀ ◖◗ ♣ P

Thatched Cottage
Emmbrook Road (off A329)
☎ (0118) 978 2552
11.45-3, 5.30-11; 12-3, 7-10.30 (Sun)
Morland Original; guest beer Ⓗ
Traditional country pub with one bar and restaurant area. Thick carpet, copper fire hood and a welcoming atmosphere. No food Mon. *Recommended.*
◗ P

Three Brewers ⓭
Barkham Road
☎ (0118) 979 5564
11-11; 12-10.30 (Sun)
Ushers Best, seasonal beers Ⓗ
Lively locals' pub close to station, just across level crossing from town. Darts and Aunt Sally teams. Juke box and small patio area at rear.

'There are two reasons for drinking: one is when you are thirsty to cure it; the other when you are not thirsty to prevent it… Prevention is better than cure'

Thomas Love Peacock (1785–1866)

Three Frogs
222 London Road (A329)
☎ (0118) 978 5925
11-11; 12-10.30 (Sun)
Ruddles County; Morland Original, Old Speckled Hen, seasonal beers Ⓗ
Large Morland Artist's Fare pub with two separate bars and restaurant area. Plenty of outside seating. Food available all day. *Recommended.*
❀ ◖◗ ⊞ ♣ P

Two Poplars
118 Finchampstead Road (B3016)
☎ (0118) 978 0590
11-11; 12-10.30 (Sun)
Ruddles County; Morland Original, seasonal beers Ⓗ
Named after trees planted in front of pub when opened in 1926 but replanted after storms in 1993. Large two-bar family pub with conservatory and garden. Large screen TV, pool table and juke box. Food available 11–2.30, 7–9. *Recommended.*
❀ ◖◗ P

Victoria Arms
1 Easthampstead Road
No Real Ale.

White Horse
Easthampstead Road (1 mile south-east of town)
☎ (0118) 978 1025
11-11; 12-10.30 (Sun)
Morland Independent IPA, Original, Old Speckled Hen; Ruddles Best Ⓗ
Large smart lounge bar with Morland dray theme in keeping with the pub's name. Bar billiards table. Disabled access (front door) and toilets. Small secluded garden at rear.

Woodley F3

An eastern suburb of Reading.

Bull & Chequers
Church Road, Woodley Green
☎ (0118) 969 9756
11-11; 12-10.30 (Sun)
Courage Best, Directors; Greene King IPA, Abbot Ⓗ
Originally a farmhouse when Woodley was in the countryside. Large garden with children's play area; paved patio at the front.

Chequers
198 Crockhamwell Road
☎ (0118) 969 2171
11-11; 12-10.30 (Sun)
Courage Best; Theakston XB Ⓗ
Busy town pub in Woodley shopping precinct. Pool table.

Good Companions
149 Loddon Bridge Road
☎ (0118) 969 3325
11-11; 12-10.30 (Sun)
Courage Best Ⓗ
Modern, two-bar pub. Large lounge has separate dining area and the small public bar can get smoky. Good value food.

Inn on the Park
The Pavilion, Woodford Park, Haddon Drive
☎ (0118) 962 8655
11-11; 11-3, 6-11 (Mon, Wed, Thur); 12-10.30 (Sun)
Brakspear Bitter, Brakspear Special; guest beers Ⓗ
Owned by Woodley town council as part of its sports centre. Outside patio next to tennis courts, bowling and putting greens, paddling pools, etc. Meeting room available. *Recommended.*
❀ ♿ ♣ P

Shepherds House
London Road (A4)
No Real Ale.

Thatchers
Fairwater Drive
☎ (0118) 926 7846
11-11; 12-10.30 (Sun)
Courage Best, Directors; Theakston Best; guest beers Ⓗ
Modern, neat one-bar pub with thatched roof. Recently re-thatched after disastrous fire.

Woodley Yeoman
Howth Drive
☎ (0118) 926 1810
11-11; 12-10.30 (Sun)
Whitbread Trophy Ⓗ
Two-bar, spacious modern community pub with comfortable lounge. Pool and darts. Cheap beer but served through sparkler.

Woodside H3

A pleasant rural area of Winkfield.

Duke Of Edinburgh
Woodside (off A332 signed Woodside, OS 927708)
☎ (01344) 882736
11-3, 5-11; 12-10.30 (Sun)
Arkell's 2B, 3B, Kingsdown Ⓗ
Old, semi-open-plan building with comfortable furnishings and Chelsea FC pictures. Rare outlet for Arkell's beers in east Berkshire. Hard to find but close to Ascot racecourse, with prices to match. Separate restaurant (book). *Recommended.*
🏠 ❀ ◐ ♣ P

Rose & Crown
Woodside Road (near A332, OS 929712)
☎ (01344) 882051
12-11; closed Sun eve
Morland Original; Charles Wells Bombardier; Adnams Broadside; guest beer Ⓗ
Small pub hidden in country lane, noted for its food. Billed as 'traditional pub restaurant'. Closes Sun once lunchtime diners have left. Alterations planned to provide disabled toilets. *Recommended.*
❀ 🛏 ◐ P

Woodspeen B3

Five Bells
Lambourn Road (OS 451687)
☎ (01635) 48763
11-11, 12-10.30 (Sun)
Ruddles Best; **Flowers** Original; **Charles Wells** Bombardier; guest beer Ⓗ
One-bar rural pub with separate dining area. Bar snacks available every lunchtime and evening. Sunday roasts. Ideal for Lambourn Valley or nearby Watermill Theatre.
Recommended.
Q ❀ 🛏 ◐◑ ♿ ♣ P ⊬

Woolhampton D3

On the canal, A4 Bath–London road and railway (note that the station is actually called Midgham).

Angel
Bath Road (A4)
☎ (0118) 971 3307
11-3, 6-11; 12-3, 6-10.30 (Sun)
Flowers Original; **Boddingtons** Bitter; **Brakspear** Bitter Ⓗ
Impressive ivy-clad exterior and a tidy, parquet floored interior with separate restaurant. Mixed clientele but predominantly thirtysomethings. Restaurant menu or bar snacks.

Falmouth Arms
Bath Road (A4)
☎ (0118) 971 3202
11-11; 12-10.30 (Sun)
Draught **Bass**; **Thomas Hardy** Country Ⓗ
Comfortable roadside locals' pub convenient for passing trade as it is open all day. Meals served every lunchtime and evening. Outside patio.
Recommended.
⛫ ❀ 🛏 ◐◑ ≹ ♣ P

Rising Sun, Woolhampton

Rising Sun

Bath Road (A4)
☎ (0118) 971 2717
11-3, 6-11; 12-3, 7-10.30 (Sun)
Thomas Hardy Royal Oak, Country, Pope's; Draught Bass Ⓗ
Comfortable roadside pub with bar and two dining areas, one no-smoking. Meals served every lunchtime and evening.
Recommended.
⛫Q❀◐◑♿P⚟

Row Barge Inn

Station Road (off A4)
☎ (0118) 971 2213
11-3, 6-11; 12-3, 6-10.30 (Sun)
Courage Best; Fuller's London Pride; Marston's Pedigree; Wadworth 6X; Rebellion IPA Ⓗ
Well-appointed inn beside Kennet and Avon canal. Popular with hikers and boaters alike. Lovely canalside gardens; ideal for families. Meals served every lunchtime and evening.
Recommended.
⛫Q❀◐◑♿⇄♣P

Wraysbury J3

Formerly in Buckinghamshire, this riverside village was once the site of a Benedictine nunnery where Henry VIII courted Anne Boleyn.

George

29 Windsor Road
☎ (01784) 482407
11-3, 6-11; 12-3, 7-10.30 (Sun)
Courage Best, Directors; Fuller's London Pride Ⓗ
Small drinking area in the front of this otherwise mainly food-based pub.

Perseverance

High Street
☎ (01784) 482375
11-11; 12-4, 7-10.30 (Sun)
Courage Best, Directors Ⓗ
Small locals' bar is situated on the left of pub while the rest is turned over to food.

Yattendon D2

The village has an attractive market place with wisteria and vine covered cottages, and was the home of Robert Bridges, the poet laureate, for 22 years.

The church was built by Sir John Norreys circa 1450. He was beheaded after being accused of having an affair with Anne Boleyn.

Royal Oak

The Square (OS 552745)
☎ (01635) 201325
11-3, 6-11; 12-3, 7-10.30 (Sun)
Fuller's London Pride; West Berkshire Good Old Boy Ⓗ
Attractive 16th-century village inn offering accommodation. Separate restaurant.

'Yes, my soul sentimentally craves British Beer'

Thomas Campbell (Epistle from Algiers)

Joining CAMRA

To join CAMRA, all you need to do is complete the application form opposite and send it to:

CAMRA
230 Hatfield Road
St. Albans
Hertfordshire
AL1 4LW

CAMRA contacts

The three branch contacts for Berkshire are:

- *West Berkshire*
  Clive Stevens: (01488) 683398
- *Reading & Mid-Berkshire*
  Janet Blurton: (0118) 961 9140
- *Slough, Windsor & Maidenhead*
  Vic Powell: (01753) 735765

Free updates to this guide (see page 135 for further details):

- *E-mail*
  berkshire.pubs@virgin.net

National contact points are:

- *CAMRA action line*
  0845 60 30 20 8
- *E-mail*
  camra@camra.org.uk
- *Web*
  http://www.camra.org.uk

Application form

I/We wish to join the Campaign for Real Ale and agree to abide by its rules

Title .... **Surname** ....

Forename(s) ....

Date of birth ....

Address ....

....

....

Postcode ....

Telephone number(s) ....

Date ....

Single membership	**£14**	❑
Under 26 or Over 60 (Retired)	**£8**	❑
Resident outside the European Union	**£18**	❑
Partner at the same address	add **£3**	❑

Partner's name ....

Partner's date of birth ....

Life membership and concessionary rates on request

DONATIONS WELCOME **£** ....

Payment methods

I enclose a cheque to the value **£** ....
(payable to CAMRA)

or

Please charge my Access/Mastercard/Visa/Delta/Switch

Number..

Name on card ....

Expiry date .... Issue no (Switch) ....

Signature ....
(or phone 01727 867201 with your card details)

For details of Direct Debit payments please phone:
01727 867201

(the return address for this form is given on page 126)

Tick this box if you do not wish to receive mailings from similar groups ❑

Source: Berkshire Pub Guide

County map

The county map of Berkshire is shown over the following four pages. Every village and town in the guide has a reference which may be found on this map.

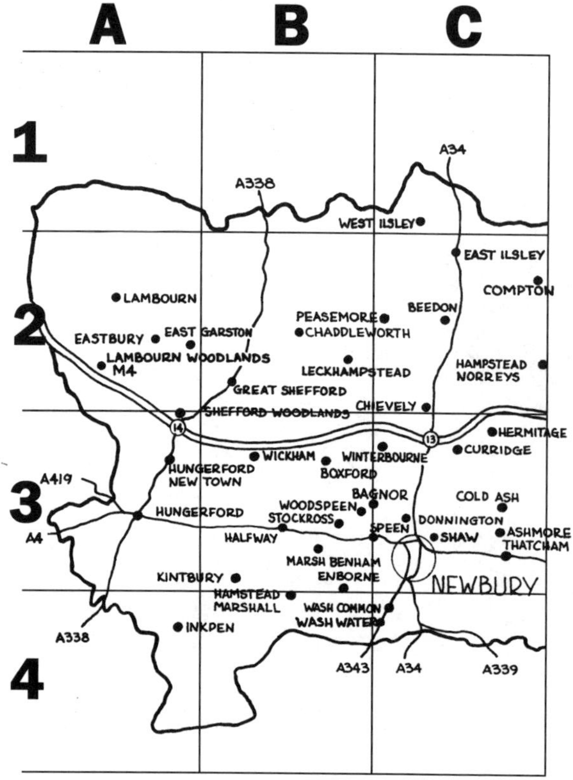
A
B
C
1
2
3
4
A34
A338
WEST ILSLEY
EAST ILSLEY
COMPTON
LAMBOURN
BEEDON
PEASEMORE
CHADDLEWORTH
EASTBURY
EAST GARSTON
LAMBOURN WOODLANDS
M4
LECKHAMPSTEAD
HAMPSTEAD NORREYS
GREAT SHEFFORD
CHIEVELY
SHEFFORD WOODLANDS
14
13
HERMITAGE
CURRIDGE
WICKHAM
WINTERBOURNE
HUNGERFORD NEW TOWN
BOXFORD
A419
BAGNOR
COLD ASH
WOODSPEEN
HUNGERFORD
STOCKROSS
DONNINGTON
A4
SPEEN
HALFWAY
SHAW
ASHMORE
THATCHAM
MARSH BENHAM
KINTBURY
ENBORNE
NEWBURY
HAMSTEAD MARSHALL
WASH COMMON
WASH WATERS
A338
INKPEN
A343
A34
A339

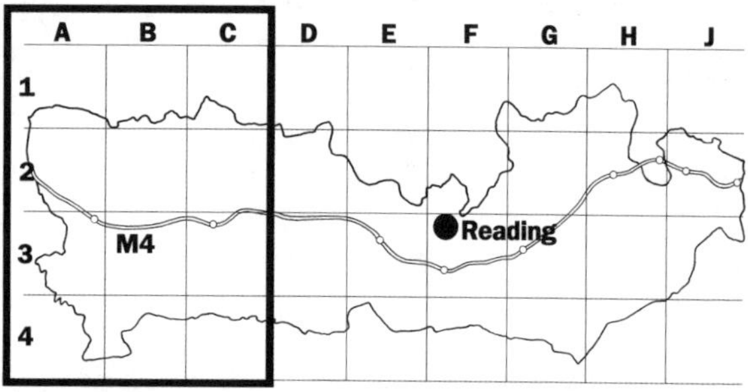
A
B
C
D
E
F
G
H
J
1
2
3
4
M4
Reading

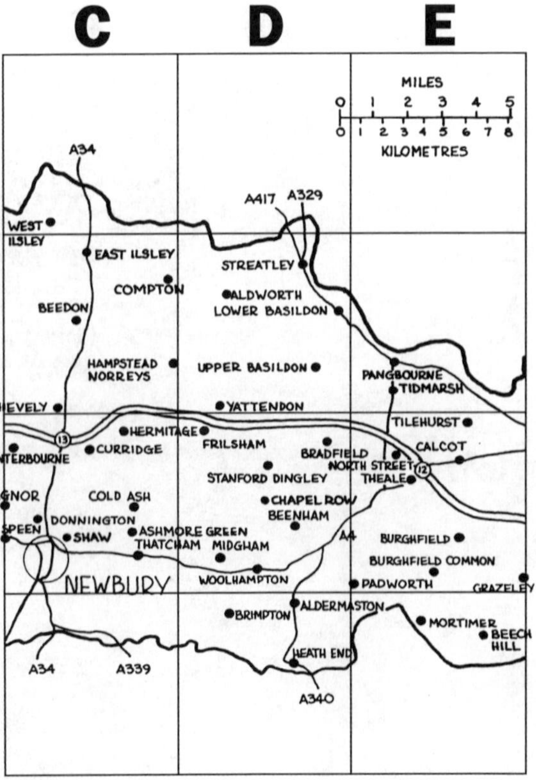
C
D
E
MILES
0 1 2 3 4 5
0 1 2 3 4 5 6 7 8
KILOMETRES
A34
A417
A329
WEST ILSLEY
EAST ILSLEY
STREATLEY
COMPTON
ALDWORTH
LOWER BASILDON
BEEDON
HAMPSTEAD NORREYS
UPPER BASILDON
PANGBOURNE
TIDMARSH
CHIEVELY
YATTENDON
TILEHURST
HERMITAGE
13
FRILSHAM
WINTERBOURNE
CURRIDGE
BRADFIELD
CALCOT
NORTH STREET
12
STANFORD DINGLEY
THEALE
BAGNOR
COLD ASH
CHAPEL ROW
BEENHAM
DONNINGTON
SPEEN
SHAW
ASHMORE GREEN
A4
BURGHFIELD
THATCHAM
MIDGHAM
BURGHFIELD COMMON
NEWBURY
WOOLHAMPTON
PADWORTH
GRAZELEY
ALDERMASTON
BRIMPTON
MORTIMER
BEECH HILL
HEATH END
A34
A339
A340

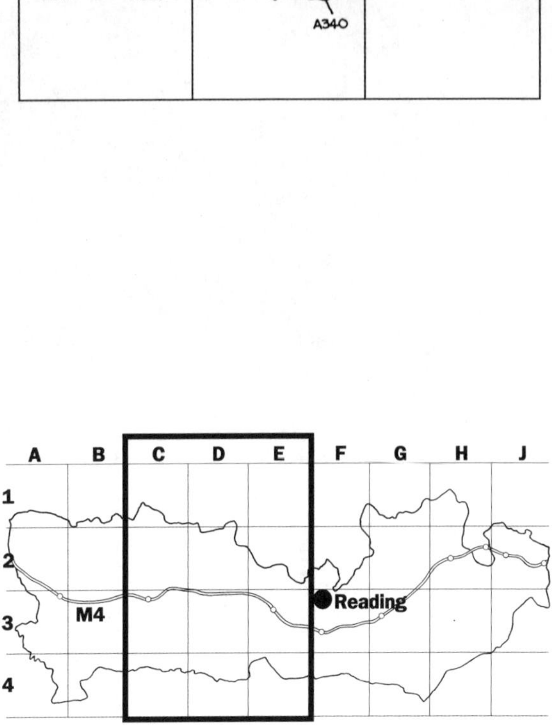
A B C D E F G H J
1
2
3
4
M4
Reading

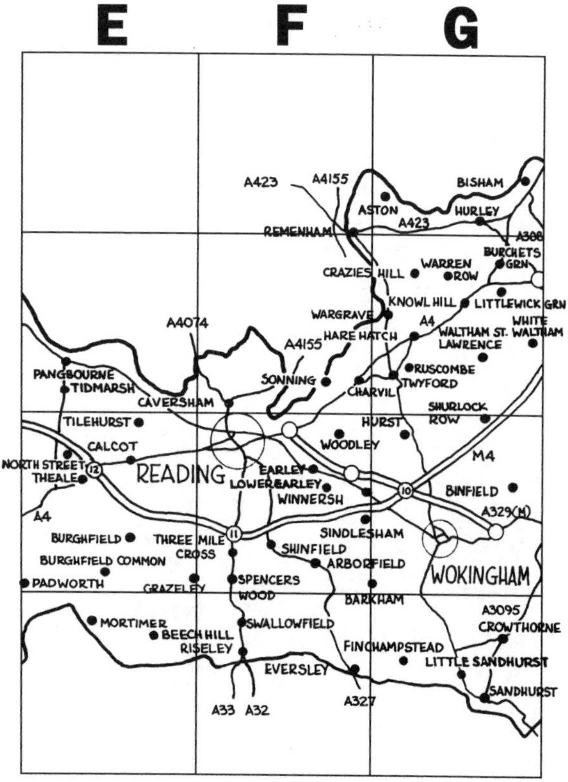
E
F
G
A423
A4155
BISHAM
ASTON
HURLEY
A423
REMENHAM
A308
BURCHETS GRN
WARREN ROW
CRAZIES HILL
KNOWL HILL
LITTLEWICK GRN
WARGRAVE
A4074
A4
WHITE WALTHAM
WALTHAM ST. LAWRENCE
HARE HATCH
A4155
RUSCOMBE
PANGBOURNE
TIDMARSH
SONNING
CHARVIL
TWYFORD
CAVERSHAM
SHURLOCK ROW
TILEHURST
HURST
CALCOT
WOODLEY
M4
NORTH STREET
THEALE
READING
EARLEY
LOWER EARLEY
WINNERSH
BINFIELD
A4
A329(M)
SINDLESHAM
BURGHFIELD
THREE MILE CROSS
SHINFIELD
BURGHFIELD COMMON
ARBORFIELD
WOKINGHAM
PADWORTH
GRAZELEY
SPENCERS WOOD
BARKHAM
A3095
MORTIMER
SWALLOWFIELD
CROWTHORNE
BEECH HILL
RISELEY
FINCHAMPSTEAD
LITTLE SANDHURST
EVERSLEY
SANDHURST
A327
A33
A32

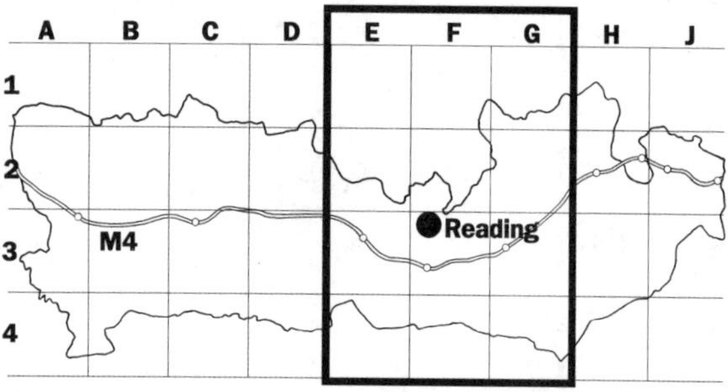
A
B
C
D
E
F
G
H
J
1
2
3
4
M4
Reading

G
H
J
1
2
3
4
A404
A4094
COOKHAM
BISHAM
COOKHAM DEAN
ASTON
HURLEY
A423
PINKNEYS GRN.
A308
MAIDENHEAD
A335
A412
BURCHETS GRN.
CRAZIES HILL
WARREN ROW
A4
CIPPENHAM
SALT HILL
SLOUGH
KNOWL HILL
LITTLEWICK GRN.
COX GRN.
BRAY
CHALVEY
WARGRAVE
HARE HATCH
WALTHAM ST. LAWRENCE
WHITE WALTHAM
ETON WICK
LANGLEY
HOLYPORT
WATER OAKLEY
ETON
TOUCHEN END
FIFIELD
DATCHET
RUSCOMBE
TWYFORD
MONEYROW GREEN
OAKLEY GRN.
COLNBROOK
HORTON
PALEY STREET
WINDSOR
SHURLOCK ROW
HURST
OLD WINDSOR
WRAYSBURY
M4
WINKFIELD
A332
WARFIELD
A308
BINFIELD
WOODSIDE
A329(M)
BRACKNELL
ASCOT
A329
SUNNINGHILL
SUNNINGDALE
BARKHAM
WOKINGHAM
A3095
A330
CROWTHORNE
A322
FINCHAMPSTEAD
LITTLE SANDHURST
MILES
SANDHURST
0 1 2 3 4 5
0 1 2 3 4 5 6 7 8
A321
KILOMETRES

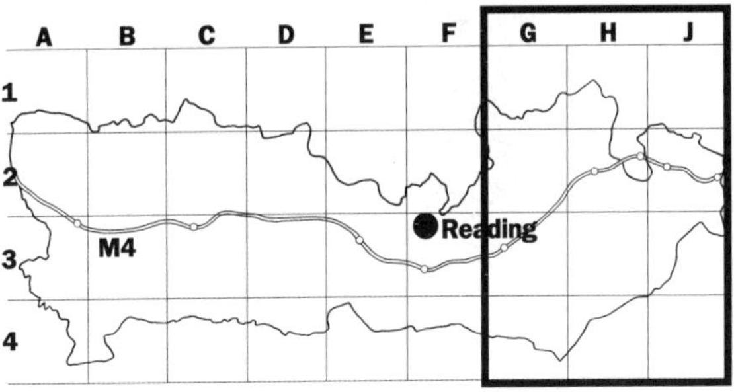
A
B
C
D
E
F
G
H
J
1
2
3
4
M4
Reading

Mmmm...

Majestically Masterful; Momentously Mature; Magically Memorable; Mightily Merrimaking; Miraculously Mysterious; Monumentally Moreish; Monsterously Misunderstood; Mean, Moody, Mellow; Made Marvellously Malty; Meritously Momentous; Mountainously Mouth-Moistening; Money Miserly; Much Maligned; Mystifyingly Murky; Masterfully Matchless; Maximum Mystique;

MAGIC!

Moreover, Merely Magnificent.

My Motto: "Make Mine Mild"

Stop press

Changes received as guide went to press:

Beech Hill, Old Elm Tree
Beech Hill Road
The speculation over this pub has sadly turned into reality with news that it is to be closed for conversion to housing, but at an uncertain date.

Bracknell, Golden Farmer
Reed's Hill (near A322), Easthampstead
Now owned by Greene King.

Maidenhead, Jack of Both Sides
81 Queen Street
Now called Bar Metro.

Reading, Greyhound
4 Mount Pleasant
Bought by developers and due to close.

Reading, Queen's Arms
24 Great Knolly's Street
Closed – future uncertain.

Windsor, Olde King & Castle
Thames Street
11-11; 12-10.30 (Sun)
Wadworth's 6X
Now open following refurbishment.

Windsor, Swan
49 Thames Street (not the Swan in Clewer village)
Closed – future uncertain.

Comments/updates

We have tried to ensure that the information in this guide is as accurate as possible, but changes are inevitable.
If you have any comments on the entries, if you discover any changes to the pubs listed, or if you would like to receive free updates, please e-mail us at:

berkshire.pubs@virgin.net

Notes

Treasures in the darkness